CAMBRIDGE O LEVEL

ENGLISH

CAMBRIDGE O LEVEL

ENGLISH

JOHN REYNOLDS ◦ PATRICIA ACRES

Orders: please contact Bookpoint Ltd, 130 Park Drive, Milton Park, Abingdon, Oxon OX14 4SE. Telephone: (44) 01235 827720. Fax: (44) 01235 400454. Email education@bookpoint.co.uk Lines are open from 9 a.m. to 5 p.m., Monday to Saturday, with a 24-hour message answering service. You can also order through our website: www.hoddereducation.com

ISBN: **9781471868634**

First published in 2016 by
Hodder Education,
An Hachette UK Company
Carmelite House
50 Victoria Embankment
London EC4Y 0DZ

www.hoddereducation.com

Impression number 10 9 8 7 6 5 4 3 2 1

Year 2020 2019 2018 2017 2016

Typeset in India by Integra Ltd

Printed in Italy

A catalogue record for this title is available from the British Library.

CONTENTS

INTRODUCTION

For the teacher

This book is intended for use by students preparing for the Cambridge International Examinations O Level English Language syllabus (1123).

The aim of the book is to present comprehensive coverage of the syllabus in a readable and interesting style that will appeal to the full range of abilities. It provides advice and practice exercises relating to the two main areas of study that are tested, which are:

- Reading
- Writing.

More detailed introductory comments about each of these main areas can be found in Chapter 1 of this book.

Despite the book's overall focus on the Cambridge O Level English Language examination, it is also hoped to provide a comprehensive course in key aspects of reading and writing English for all students in the years immediately preceding the Cambridge O Level examination. It is hoped that English lessons in the final years of a student's education will not focus solely on preparing for the terminal examination through repeated practice at answering specimen examination questions. So although this book contains many exercises which will allow students to practise the types of questions that they are likely to meet in a Cambridge O Level English Language examination, it also contains other material which is intended to allow them to develop their close reading skills to the full. One way in which this has been done is by presenting some reading passages that are longer and more detailed than those which may be found in a Reading paper of a Cambridge O Level examination (for example, on pages 66–70). The summary tasks based on these passages, as a result, may require responses longer than those stipulated in the rubric of an examination question. It is hoped that this will allow teachers to help their students to develop to the full the skills required for examination success through close consideration of the content of the passages and the precise requirements of a full answer to the questions.

Passages and questions that require longer responses than those expected for an examination answer have been flagged as Extension tasks; by answering these with care and detail, students will be exercising and becoming familiar with the very skills that will enable them to achieve the highest examination grades of which they are capable. Teachers are encouraged to engage with their students through discussing the requirements of these questions and giving guidance as to how to approach them in the classroom before asking the students to write their own answers. It is suggested that the lengthier passages relating to the Extension tasks should be treated as resource material and that teachers select from and edit this material to best suit the ability of their students.

For the student

How to use this book

Each chapter includes a variety of exercises aimed at reinforcing and testing your learning and, in particular, your ability to read for understanding and to express your ideas and understanding in written English. Your teachers may specify which elements they want you to do, but you may also want to tackle others as additional practice.

The final chapter focuses on preparing you for an examination. Although it is at the end of the book, you should read it before working through the chapters and then read it again at the end of your course of study. This chapter contains advice to follow throughout your studies, as well as guiding you through the final preparations for your examination.

1 THE O LEVEL EXAMINATION

Format and content of the examination

Cambridge O Level English Language is an untiered examination available to students throughout the world. There are different syllabuses: 1123 is available to students anywhere in the world. Other syllabuses are specific to different geographical areas.

The basic principles that underlie the 1123 syllabus are reflected in the Assessment Objectives on which the questions in the papers are based. These Assessment Objectives highlight the key skills required by all candidates taking examinations in English Language at Secondary 2 level. The details below and the practice examination-style paper at the end of the book (pages 159–65) are focused on the 1123 syllabus but the skills being assessed are common to nearly all English examinations at this level and are concerned with testing students' reading and writing. The Assessment Objectives (AOs) specific to this syllabus are as follows:

AO1: Reading

R1 Demonstrate understanding of explicit meanings
R2 Demonstrate understanding of implicit meanings and attitudes
R3 Analyse, evaluate and develop facts, ideas and opinions
R4 Demonstrate understanding of how writers achieve effects
R5 Select for specific purposes

AO2: Writing

W1 Articulate experience and express what is thought, felt and imagined
W2 Sequence facts, ideas and opinions
W3 Use a range of appropriate vocabulary
W4 Use register appropriate to audience and context
W5 Make accurate use of spelling, punctuation and grammar

Content of the examination

The Writing Paper

[1 hour 30 minutes, external examination worth 60 marks in total and 50 per cent of the qualification]

The prime purpose of this paper is to test writing skills.

Section 1: Directed Writing

Section 1 is a Directed Writing task worth 30 marks (15 marks for task fulfilment and 15 marks for language). It tests all five Writing AOs as well as Reading AO1 and AO2. Students are presented with **one** task only, related to the world of study, work or the community and are required to respond to it in a specific genre (for example letter, speech, report, article) that is fit for the stated purpose and for the stated audience. Students are expected to write between 200 and 300 words.

Section 2: Composition

Section 2 of the question paper requires students to respond to a Composition task and offers a choice of five composition topics. There may be one descriptive, two argumentative and two narrative titles from which students should choose **one** only. They should write between 350 and 500 words. This question is also worth a maximum of 30 marks, and content and language are assessed together. Linguistic accuracy is a key element of assessment. All five Writing AOs are tested.

The Reading Paper

[1 hour 45 minutes, external examination worth 50 marks in total and 50 per cent of the qualification]

The prime purpose of this paper is to test reading.

Section 1: Reading for Ideas

In Section 1, students are required to scan a factual text (or texts) of approximately 700 words (for example report(s), article(s), advertisement(s), email(s) or letter(s)). They then identify and note down information required by the questions, for example similarities and differences, causes and effects, advantages and disadvantages, problems and solutions, actions and consequences, etc. A total of 12 marks will be allocated for these content points and example content points will be given as guidance to students.

Students are then required to use their notes to write a summary of between 150 and 180 words.

Up to 10 marks are allocated for responses to the summary dependent on relevance and coherence. This task tests the AOs R5, W2 and W3.

Students are next required to answer questions to identify examples of a function in the text, for example opinions, advice, criticism or warnings. These will be short-answer questions worth 3 marks that test AO R3.

Section 2: Reading for Meaning

In Section 2, students are required to read one narrative passage (for example a report, article or story) of approximately 700 words and then respond to short-answer and multiple-choice questions testing their ability to understand the language (both explicit and implicit meanings). This tests AOs R1, R2, R3 and R4. A total of 25 marks are allocated for this section.

As you will have realised, the information given above covers only the Assessment Objectives for Writing and Reading. In the 1123 syllabus, there are no Speaking and Listening components and so in this book we are dealing only with reading and writing. Although these two skills are interdependent, we have focused on them separately in the same way that the examination includes both a Writing and a Reading paper. It is important to remember, however, that it is necessary to *read* carefully the wording of essay questions, especially the Directed Writing question, in the Writing Paper and to *write* your answers to the comprehension questions, especially the summary question, in the Reading Paper fluently and carefully in order to achieve the highest grades of which you are capable.

Key reading skills

Throughout our lives, we are continually practising our reading skills, even, at times, when we are not conscious that we are doing so. For example, when we read direction boards on a bus or check the opening times written on the doors of shops we are engaging in a form of reading in order to gain essential information. At other times, we may make a conscious decision to sit down and practise our reading, for example when we read the latest novel written by our favourite author, or look at features such as film reviews in a magazine or online.

These are just a few examples of when we engage in reading – throughout any day, most people will be involved in reading for a variety of purposes. Some of these, such as checking the opening times of a store, are what are described as passive reading; in other words, we are simply absorbing information without having to think deeply about it. However, other activities, such as reading a controversial article in a newspaper or understanding the complexities of a Science textbook, involve exercising our active reading skills, when we have to think carefully in order to understand or evaluate exactly what the writer is saying to us. The O Level examination, in particular, contains reading passages to test your active reading capabilities; but you should, nevertheless, be prepared to practise all types of reading as thoughtfully as you can.

The following are the most common types of reading activities in which we are engaged at different times:

1 Reading factual texts

Such texts will include informative/instructional texts such as handbooks telling us how to use items of electrical equipment, timetables, posters and advertisements telling us about upcoming events and so on. When we are reading items such as these, we are very much concerned with reading to gain essential information and with the intention of identifying facts and key points.

2 Reading non-fiction descriptive texts

Non-fiction texts are those that contain true accounts or factual information and include such things as biographies, guidebooks, academic writing such as school textbooks, historical accounts, etc.

3 Reading media texts

A media text is something written in a non-book medium, for example a newspaper or a website. The content can be of any type, informative, non-fiction or literary, but very often a media text is written with the intention of persuading the reader to share or be converted to a particular point of view. For example, newspaper articles that set out to convince the reader of the rightness of a particular argument; advertisements that are aimed at persuading their readers to purchase a particular commodity; websites attempting to promote a particular belief or outlook. Remember that such texts typically include graphic materials (such as photographs, diagrams and so on) to help convey their message, rather than just as illustrations. This can make them seem more convincing.

4 Reading literary texts

Literary texts are those that are written to entertain and engage the reader and consist of poems, novels, short stories and literary non-fiction texts (such as travel writing and autobiography) and drama texts.

Depending on the type of text we are reading, we adopt a slightly different approach to it; however, our main aim, whatever we are reading, is to gather information and to understand fully and evaluate what we read.

Key writing skills

Using our writing skills corresponds to using our active reading skills. As with reading, we write for a range of purposes and use a range of styles depending on the type of writing in which we are engaging. We write in order to convey information and thoughts to other people and whenever we engage in this activity it is important that we keep the purpose of our writing and the reader(s) for whom it is intended clearly in mind. We should aim to ensure that the vocabulary we use is both precise and accessible to the persons for whom we are writing. For example, if we are writing with the main purpose of providing information, we should aim to make what we write as unambiguous as possible; on the other hand, if we are writing to influence a reader's feelings, then the language we use is likely to be more complex and provoke a greater range of responses. It is also important that we adapt the tone of our writing to match the person to whom it is addressed; for example, you are likely to write quite formally if you are producing a report for your headteacher but much more informally if you are writing a letter to a good friend who has just gone away to college.

The following are the most common types of writing activities in which we are engaged at different times:

1 Writing to inform, explain or advise

Such writing includes giving instructions, such as how to cook a favourite meal; giving written directions for how to travel from one place to another; giving advice about how to care for a newly acquired pet and so on. As with reading to inform, the key point to remember here is that the primary intention of such writing is to convey facts and details as clearly as possible.

2 Writing to describe

Descriptive writing can be either factual or imaginative or both together. For example, if you are writing a description of your school or college with the intention of providing a guide to it for a new student, then it is important that you describe the place factually with as much detail and clarity as you can. However, if you are required by your English teacher to describe a place that you find terrifying and decide that your school building would be a good subject to choose, then you should try to use language in as imaginative a way as you can in order to emphasise the terrifying aspects of the building!

3 Writing to argue or persuade

Both of these types of writing require you to use facts and opinions but to express them in such a way that you can use them to encourage your reader(s) to share your point of view. The language you use, therefore, will be more complex and emotively toned than what you would use if you were simply writing to convey information or instructions.

4 Writing to analyse, review or comment

When you write analytically, you are likely to be considering an argument put forward by another writer and commenting on its strengths and weaknesses. Another type of analytical writing is when you are reviewing a piece of literature you have read, a film or television programme you have seen or a piece of music you have heard, and are explaining what was good or bad about it. Yet another type of writing which fits into this category would be a report on a sporting fixture in which you explain who played well and who played badly and dissect mistakes made by the teams, which led to the particular outcome of the match.

5 Writing to explore, entertain or reflect

This category of writing is intended to provide pleasure for the reader and involves writing personally about your experiences. In doing so, you are likely to convey your thoughts and feelings about a particular topic, person or place and to describe it in an original and interesting way. For example, you may be writing about a particular episode in your life that had an important effect on your development as an individual or writing about a certain place you visited, which left a lasting impression on you. Poetry is, of course, another type of writing that gives pleasure to the reader.

6 Writing to imagine

This category of writing is also intended to provide pleasure for the reader but differs from the previous category because, although what you are writing may be based on your personal experience, it has been turned into a piece of fiction which involves imagined characters and imaginary settings. Such writing includes novels and short stories.

7 Directed or transactional writing

This is not really a separate category of writing, but is how a part of an English examination paper is often presented. The task involves both reading and writing skills as you are provided with a series of details and then asked to use them in a piece of writing which is intended for a specific purpose. For example, you may be given a series of details relating to a forthcoming school event, such as an open evening, and be asked to write a letter to parents informing them of what will be involved in the open evening, what time it starts and so on. Or the letter might need to be addressed to your aunt, persuading her to come to see you act in the play that is part of the evening's events.

Standard English

When you are writing anything specifically related to assessment for an O Level English Language examination it is very important that you communicate by using Standard English. This does not mean that you have to use an exceptionally old-fashioned and over-formal mode of expression but that you should pay particular care to the accepted conventions of English expression, spelling, punctuation and grammatical usage which are common to those who use English as a written and spoken medium throughout the whole world. Whereas colloquialisms and dialect terms are perfectly acceptable when speaking with, writing to or texting friends of your own age group, when communicating with people of an older generation or with those who live in a different country – and teachers often fall into both of those categories! – it is essential that you adopt the form of language which is likely to be familiar to them. There will be sections in the chapters throughout this book that will focus on the key aspects of accurate Standard English expression.

The chapters in this book will deal with the different types of reading and writing skills through different text types.

Reading information and instructions

Read these pieces of writing carefully and then decide what they have in common:

Text 1

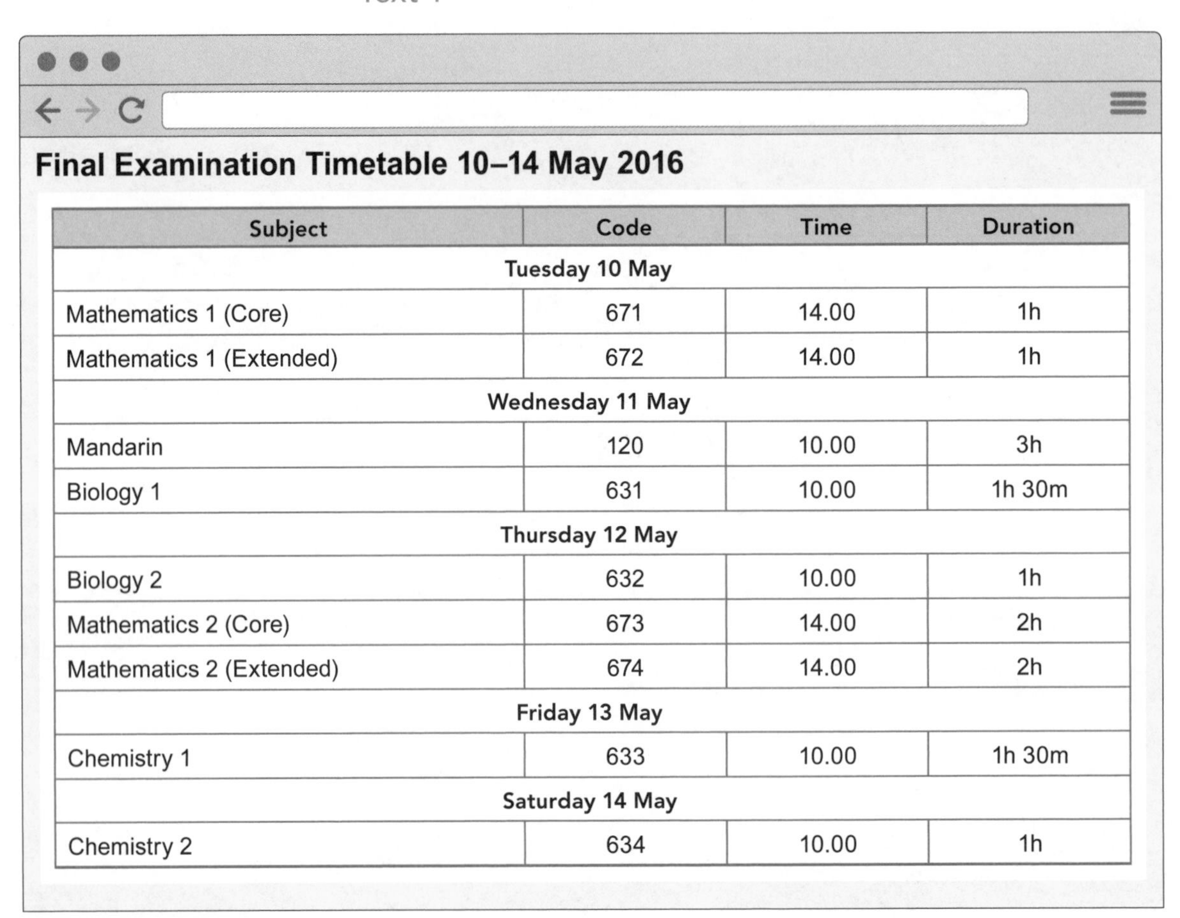

Final Examination Timetable 10–14 May 2016

Subject	Code	Time	Duration
Tuesday 10 May			
Mathematics 1 (Core)	671	14.00	1h
Mathematics 1 (Extended)	672	14.00	1h
Wednesday 11 May			
Mandarin	120	10.00	3h
Biology 1	631	10.00	1h 30m
Thursday 12 May			
Biology 2	632	10.00	1h
Mathematics 2 (Core)	673	14.00	2h
Mathematics 2 (Extended)	674	14.00	2h
Friday 13 May			
Chemistry 1	633	10.00	1h 30m
Saturday 14 May			
Chemistry 2	634	10.00	1h

Text 2

Getting started with your MP4 Digital Player

Downloading music

Before playing music on your MP4 player it is necessary to download your selected files from your computer. To do this, you should:

- connect your MP4 player to your computer
- open the music files saved on your computer (using, for example, Windows Media Player)
- Use the Synch function to transfer files between your computer and your MP4 Digital Player.

Using the Music function on your MP4 player

When you enter the Music section, you will see the Control screen.

- First, press the Play/Pause button to start the music.
- If you wish to pause the music, press the Play/Pause button again.
- To stop the music, hold down the Play/Pause button for 5 seconds.
- To move on to the next song, press the Next/Fast Forward button.
- To return to the previous song, press the Previous/Rewind button.

Text 3

Here is some general travel information and tips for visitors to Sri Lanka.

Sri Lanka Visa and Passport Requirements

	Passport required	Return ticket required	Visa required
Australian	Yes	Yes	Yes
British	Yes	Yes	Yes
Canadian	Yes	Yes	Yes
Other EU	Yes	Yes	Yes
USA	Yes	Yes	Yes

Passports

To enter Sri Lanka, passports should have one blank page and be valid for no less than six months from the date of arrival.

Visas

Visas to Sri Lanka are required by all nationals referred to in the chart above.

Tourists should apply online through the Electronic Travel Authorization System (ETA) (www.eta.gov.lk) and pay the requisite application fee. It's recommended that you apply before you travel; there is an ETA desk at the international airport where you can apply on arrival (credit cards or US dollars only), but you could be subject to long delays.

Business travellers should obtain a visa through the embassy/high commission.

Note: Nationals not referred to in the chart are advised to contact the nearest embassy or high commission to check visa requirements for Sri Lanka.

Types and cost

Transit visa: free; double-entry tourist visa (ETA): US$30 in advance or US$35 on arrival. Children under 12 are exempt from paying a visa fee for stays of up to 30 days.

➜

You can also apply for a visa through the embassy/high commission. The fees are as follows:

- Tourist visa: £35 (up to 30 days); £45 (30–90 days).
- Business visa: £45 (up to 30 days); £135 (30–90 days).

Validity

- Transit visas: two days
- Double-entry ETA tourist visa: 30 days
- Tourist visa from embassy/high commission: 30 or 90 days.

Application to

In person at the nearest consulate (or consular section of high commission/embassy) or online (www.eta.gov.lk).

Working days

The ETA tourist visa generally takes two days to come through.

If you apply through the embassy/high commission, allow four working days for visa processing.

Extension of stay

Visitors can request to extend their ETA by applying to the Department of Immigration and Emigration (www.immigration.gov.lk). This is issued at the discretion of the authorities who must be satisfied that the applicant has sufficient funds and holds an onward or return ticket for travel.

Embassies and tourist offices

High Commission of Sri Lanka in the UK

Telephone: (020) 7262 1841

Website: http://www.srilankahighcommission.co.uk/

Opening times: Mon–Fri 0930–1700; 0930–1300 (visa section)

Embassy of Sri Lanka in the USA

Telephone: (202) 483 402 528

Website: http://www.slembassyusa.org

Opening times: Mon–Fri 0900–1700

Currency & money

Currency information

Sri Lanka Rupee (LKR; symbol Rp) = 100 cents. Notes are in denominations of Rp2000, 1000, 500, 200, 100, 50, 20 and 10. Coins are in denominations of Rp10, 5, 2 and 1, and 50, 25, 10, 5, 2 and 1 cents. There are also large numbers of commemorative coins in circulation.

Credit cards

MasterCard and Visa are widely accepted. American Express is also often accepted. The tourist board urges caution when paying by credit card due to the potential for fraud.

ATM

Major cities have ATMs, although not all will accept international cards, especially the national bank. It is advisable to try to have some cash at hand while travelling, particularly in rural areas.

Traveller's cheques

Traveller's cheques are often not accepted. If you find somewhere that will exchange them, the rate of exchange for traveller's cheques can be better than the rate of exchange for cash but there are handling fees to consider and banks are more likely to give a favourable rate than hotels. To avoid additional exchange rate charges, travellers are advised to take traveller's cheques in US dollars or pounds sterling.

Banking hours

Mon–Sat 0900–1300. Some city banks close at 1500; some even have night-time banking facilities.

Currency restriction

The import and export of local currency is limited to Rp5000. The import of notes from India and Pakistan is not allowed. Otherwise, the import of foreign currency is not restricted but all amounts over US$10 000 are subject to declaration at customs. Export of foreign currency is limited to the amount declared on import.

Currency exchange

Foreign currency can be changed at authorised exchanges, banks and hotels.

http://www.worldtravelguide.net/sri-lanka/money-duty-free

Text 4

For sale

Ford Mustang

AUTOMATIC TRANSMISSION, POWER STEERING AND BRAKES.

RECENTLY COMPLETED A 6-MONTH RECONDITIONING PROGRAM, INTERIOR PANELS, 'PONY STAMP' SEATING, NEW ARW WHEELS/ TYRES, RE-SPRAY AND MUCH MORE.

NEW M.O.T.

- Engine: 5.3 Litre 289 cu. ins. V/8
- Transmission: Automatic
- Exterior: Black Clearcoat
- Interior: Red 'Pony' Stamped
- Power Steering
- Disc Braking
- 6-Month Restoration incl. New Black Roof, New 'Pony' Interior, Carpets, Floor Mats, Doortrims, Seats, etc.
- New '65 Mustang ARW Alloys, New '65 GT Grille w/Foglamps.

4,300,000.00JMD

Although their subject matter is different, the main purpose of each one of these pieces of writing is to give information. The information given in each case consists of *facts* that allow the readers to find the precise details they are looking for without distractions such as the writers' opinions about what they are describing or any other unnecessary comments.

Facts and opinions

One of the most important points to keep in mind when you are reading a piece of non-fiction writing is to distinguish between *facts* and *opinions*. A *fact* is a statement that can be verified by external evidence whereas an *opinion* is simply a statement of what a person thinks about something and cannot, therefore, be proved to be true or false. Very often people will attempt to pass off their opinions as if they are facts so it is important that you, as a reader, are alert to this practice. Here are some examples:

- The name of the main airport in Mauritius is the Sir Seewoosagur Ramgoolam International Airport; it is named in honour of a former Prime Minister of the country. (Both of these statements are facts as they can be confirmed by referring to official documents.)
- The Sir Seewoosagur Ramgoolam International Airport has more friendly staff than any other airport in the whole world. (This is clearly an opinion; it is what the speaker thinks but it cannot be proved to be true or untrue. After all, it is highly unlikely that the speaker will have visited every airport in the whole world!)

- The wide range of shopping facilities available at the Sir Seewoosagur Ramgoolam International Airport allows passengers to pass the time easily while they are waiting to board their flights. (This is an opinion disguised as a fact; it is only the writer's opinion that the range of shopping facilities on offer at the airport is wide and it is also only the writer's opinion that all passengers will want to pass their time in this way. Note that it makes no difference whether you agree with the opinion or not; you may also think that the range of shopping facilities is wide, but it is still an opinion, one that you happen to share. It can be helpful when you come across statements like this to preface them with the phrase, 'The writer thinks that ...'. If it makes sense when you do this, then the statement is likely to be an opinion.)

Examples of writing containing opinions will be considered in Chapter 4.

Types of informative writing

Now, let's look at some of the different ways in which factual information is given to people.

Timetables and travel information

One of the most common forms in which information is given is by timetables. It is important that the information they contain can be understood quickly and easily by people who may be in a hurry. There should be no chance of any misunderstanding and so the timetable must contain only essential information and be set out in such a way that it can be read and understood at a glance. For this reason, most timetables will present their information in a *tabular* format as this makes it easier for readers to identify the key points they are looking for. The timetable for the examinations as shown on page 8 is a good example of this as the key information (date, time of day, examination subject) is clearly set out with no distractions.

Exercise 1

1 You are on a touring holiday in the USA and decide to travel from New York to New Orleans by coach. You visit the website of the Greyhound bus company and find the following possible schedules for your journey. Read the table carefully and then answer the questions below.

   a Which of the schedules involves the fewest transfers?
   b Which of the schedules provides the quickest journey?
   c You wish to arrive in New Orleans in the morning but not too early. Which is the most suitable schedule for you to choose?

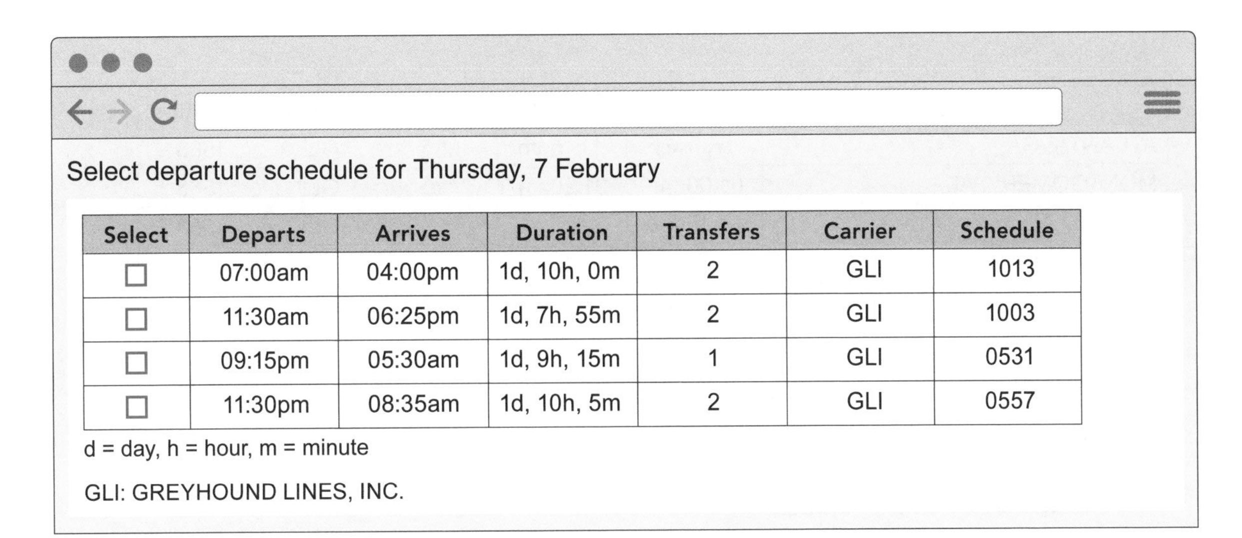
Select departure schedule for Thursday, 7 February

Select	Departs	Arrives	Duration	Transfers	Carrier	Schedule
☐	07:00am	04:00pm	1d, 10h, 0m	2	GLI	1013
☐	11:30am	06:25pm	1d, 7h, 55m	2	GLI	1003
☐	09:15pm	05:30am	1d, 9h, 15m	1	GLI	0531
☐	11:30pm	08:35am	1d, 10h, 5m	2	GLI	0557

d = day, h = hour, m = minute

GLI: GREYHOUND LINES, INC.

2 You finally decide that you will take the bus which leaves New York at 11.30 p.m. and then look at the details of the journey which are printed below. Read through these details carefully and then answer the questions that follow.

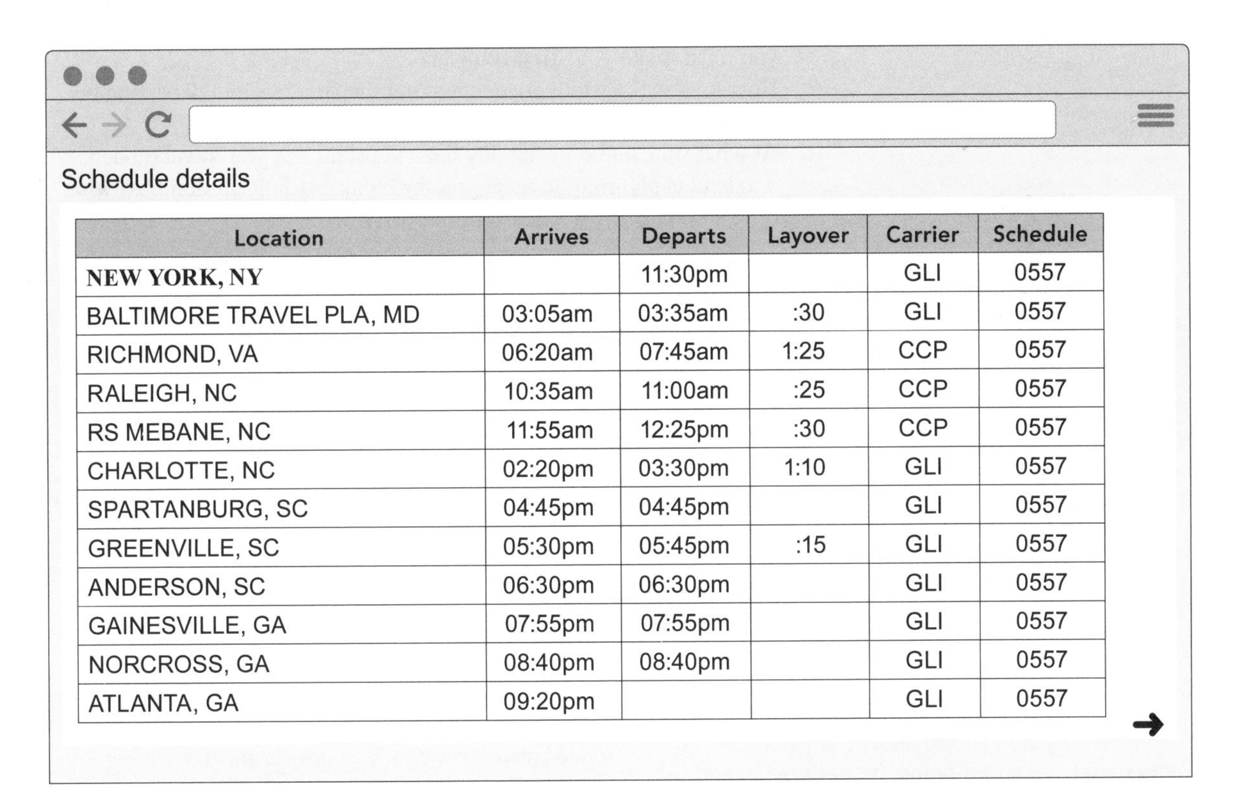
Schedule details

Location	Arrives	Departs	Layover	Carrier	Schedule
NEW YORK, NY		11:30pm		GLI	0557
BALTIMORE TRAVEL PLA, MD	03:05am	03:35am	:30	GLI	0557
RICHMOND, VA	06:20am	07:45am	1:25	CCP	0557
RALEIGH, NC	10:35am	11:00am	:25	CCP	0557
RS MEBANE, NC	11:55am	12:25pm	:30	CCP	0557
CHARLOTTE, NC	02:20pm	03:30pm	1:10	GLI	0557
SPARTANBURG, SC	04:45pm	04:45pm		GLI	0557
GREENVILLE, SC	05:30pm	05:45pm	:15	GLI	0557
ANDERSON, SC	06:30pm	06:30pm		GLI	0557
GAINESVILLE, GA	07:55pm	07:55pm		GLI	0557
NORCROSS, GA	08:40pm	08:40pm		GLI	0557
ATLANTA, GA	09:20pm			GLI	0557

→

Location	Arrives	Departs	Layover	Carrier	Schedule
ATLANTA, GA	**Transfer**	11:15pm	1:55	GLI	1563
MONTGOMERY, AL	01:00am	01:20am	:20	GLI	1563
MOBILE, AL	04:15am			GLI	1563
MOBILE, AL	**Transfer**	04:45am	:30	COP	0681
BILOXI, MS	05:55am	06:00am	:05	COP	0681
GULFPORT, MS	06:30am	06:30am		COP	0681
SLIDELL, LA	07:40am	07:40am		COP	0681
NEW ORLEANS, LA	08:35am				

GLI = GREYHOUND LINES, INC.

CCP = CAROLINA TRAILWAYS POOLED

COP = CAPITAL COLONIAL TWS POOL

a In which two towns do you have to transfer from one bus to another?
b On what day, and at what time, does the bus arrive in the town where you must make your first transfer?
c How long is the wait between leaving the first bus and departing on the next one?
d At what time and on what day does the final bus you travel on depart?
e A friend is planning to meet you for breakfast in Richmond. At what time should he be waiting for your arrival?

3 Before travelling, you consult the website again and read through the more detailed information for travellers which is printed below. Look at this information carefully and then answer the questions that follow.

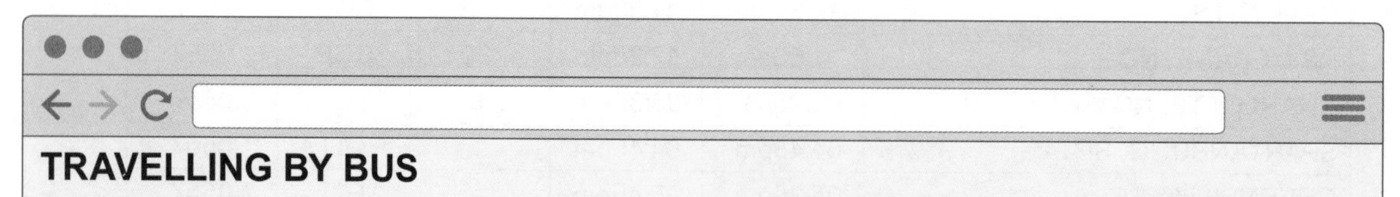

TRAVELLING BY BUS

How We Operate

No reservations are necessary when you travel with Greyhound. If you know the departure schedule, simply arrive at the terminal at least an hour before departure to purchase your ticket. Boarding generally begins 15 to 30 minutes before departure. **Seating is on a first-come, first-served basis.** Advance purchase tickets do not guarantee a seat.

When Greyhound fills a regularly scheduled bus with passengers during times of peak demand, Greyhound plans for additional buses to accommodate passengers beyond the seating capacity of a single bus for any given schedule. However, our ability to add extra sections depends on the availability of buses, drivers and the number of passengers.

When picking up passengers en route (such as at a rest stop), continuing passengers who de-boarded at the rest stop are given priority to re-board.

Greyhound buses travel around the clock, so you can travel by day and enjoy the scenery through wide panoramic windows. Or, select a night service, and relax in a reclining seat with reduced interior lighting.

Most buses make intermediate stops to pick up additional passengers en route to their destinations. In addition to stops en route, buses make rest stops every few hours, and meal stops are scheduled as close to normal meal times as possible. If you prefer not to travel on a bus that includes multiple stops en route, be sure to ask your ticket agent about our express schedules, which are available on select routes.

For information on parking at Greyhound locations, please contact the location nearest you.

Enjoy Your Trip

All Greyhound buses are equipped with air conditioning, an on-board restroom, reclining seats with headrests, footrests and tinted windows. Feel free to bring reading material, radio headsets and a small pillow for your comfort. Food and non-alcoholic beverages may be carried on board for personal consumption.

Radios, laptops and other electronic items may be carried on board, provided that they do not disturb fellow passengers and that headphones are used. (External power outlets are NOT available on Greyhound buses.) Greyhound buses are not equipped for movies on board, although some connecting carriers may offer this service.

Customers with disabilities who need travel assistance should call the Greyhound Customers with Disabilities Travel Assist line at 1-800-752-4841 at least 48 hours prior to departure.

On Board Restrictions

For everyone's safety and comfort, Greyhound asks that customers please follow certain restrictions while on board. Federal law does not permit smoking on Greyhound buses. **We have a zero tolerance for alcohol, drugs, weapons and unruly behaviour.**

Photography, video or audio recording of Greyhound personnel, equipment or procedures is strictly prohibited. For your safety and the safety of those around you, passengers should remain seated while the bus is in motion. Audio, video and camera equipment should be stored with other carry-ons when not in use.

No dogs, cats, birds, or other animals will be transported. However, a service animal, trained for the purpose of accompanying a disabled person, will be permitted to travel with the disabled person at no additional charge.

Which option is correct for each question?

a In order to buy a ticket for a Greyhound bus journey you should:
   i arrive at least an hour before the bus is scheduled to depart
   ii arrive 15 minutes before the bus is scheduled to depart
   iii ask for a particular seat on arrival
   iv reserve your seat in advance.

b All Greyhound buses:
   i are air-conditioned
   ii make stops every few hours
   iii offer movies for passengers to watch
   iv provide audio headsets for their passengers.

c All passengers on Greyhound buses are allowed to:
   i bring pets on the bus
   ii drink alcohol on board the bus
   iii eat on board the bus
   iv smoke while on the bus.

Posters and advertisements

Another very effective way of giving information is through the use of posters and advertisements in the media. Here are some examples. Example 1 is a poster relating to a campaign to stamp out bullying in schools and it sets out to describe what forms bullying can take. Example 2 comes from a campaign run by the National Health Service (NHS) in the UK in an attempt to inform parents of the benefits to children's health of encouraging them to eat more fruit and vegetables. As well as using words to convey this information, both campaigns include graphic features in their material to attract the reader's attention.

Read through both sets of material and then answer the questions that follow.

Example 1

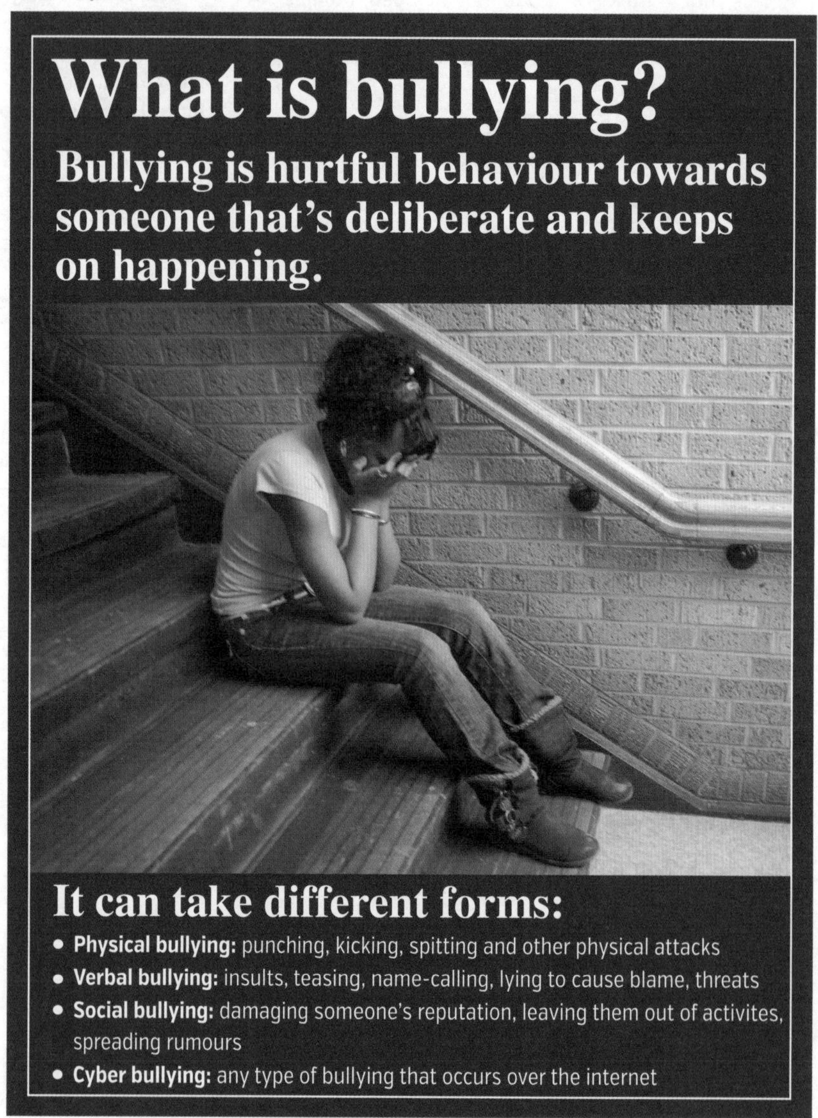

Example 2

Why eat 5 A DAY?

Fruit and vegetables help set you up for a healthier lifestyle. Best of all, there is so much variety to choose from, all year long, that there's enough to keep even the fussiest eaters happy.

To get the best health benefits, your 5 A DAY portions should include a combination of a variety of fruit and vegetables. That's 5 portions altogether, not 5 portions of fruit and 5 portions of vegetables.

Here are 5 great reasons to eat 5 portions of fruit and vegetables A DAY

- They're packed with vitamins and minerals.
- They can help you to maintain a healthy weight.
- They're an excellent source of fibre and antioxidants.
- They help reduce the risk of heart disease, stroke and some cancers.
- They taste delicious and there's so much variety to choose from.

What counts?

Almost all fruit and vegetables count towards your 5 A DAY. What's more there's no limit to how much you can consume – so the more you eat, the better. It's also good to know that you should eat a variety of fruit and vegetables to get the maximum nutritional benefits. This is because they each contain different combinations of fibre, vitamins, minerals and other nutrients. Besides, eating the same ones every day would be boring.

You probably won't have to dramatically change your diet to reach the recommended amount of fruit and vegetables you should eat. From takeaways to ready meals, fruit and vegetables can be found in many things you eat, you just need to know where to look.

HOWEVER!! Ready meals, convenience foods and takeaways are often high in added salt, sugar or fat and should only be eaten in moderation – so it's important to check the nutritional information on food labels.

Have a look at the following guidelines and you'll soon be on your way to 5 A DAY:

- Fresh, frozen, chilled, canned, 100% juice and smoothies all count, as do dried fruit and vegetables.
- Fruit and vegetables don't have to be eaten on their own to count. You can also include any vegetables found in soups, stews, sandwiches and other dishes.
- Fruit and vegetables contained in convenience foods like ready meals, pasta sauces, soups and puddings, also contribute to your 5 A DAY. However, these ready-made foods can be high in salt, sugar and fat, which should only ever be eaten in moderation, so it's important to check the nutritional information on the labels and packaging.
- Dietary supplements like vitamins and minerals do not count towards 5 A DAY. This is because many dietary supplements don't have the same nutritional benefits as fruit and vegetables.
- Potatoes and other related vegetables such as yams and cassava do not count. This is because they are classified as starchy foods.

Exercise 2

1 What makes the anti-bullying poster effective? Does the photograph add information or is it just an illustration? Explain briefly how the whole poster succeeds in attracting the reader's attention and in conveying information.
2 Write down the facts you have learnt about the importance of a balanced diet from the NHS Healthy Eating material.
3 Does the NHS material contain only facts, or can you find examples of opinions as well? Does it repeat any facts?
4 Comment on the language used in the NHS material. Do you think that it is successful in making sure that the readers understand the information clearly? Is there a part that you could have written more clearly? Give examples in your answer.

Instructions

Understanding instructions of how to perform a particular task is another important informative reading skill. If you cannot understand the instructions, then it is most likely that you will not complete the task successfully.

Exercise 3

Here is a jumbled list of instructions about how to operate the timer on a DVD recorder. The first and last points are in the correct position; rearrange the rest so that they make sense.

- Turn on television set and DVD recorder, using the remote control.
- Use the arrow keys on the remote control to change television channels.
- Scroll down and select the 'Timer' option.
- Select the number of the channel you wish to record.
- Select 'Time', 'Date', 'Channel' from the options displayed on screen.
- Press 'Menu' button on remote control to display options available.
- Press 'Enter' button on remote control to pre-set Timer recording.
- Press 'Timer' button to exit screen.
- Once all options are completed press 'OK' button on remote control.
- Now press 'Timer' button to clear screen and then press 'Standby' button to complete Timer recording.

Writing to inform and explain

The previous section of this chapter gave you the opportunity to study and analyse some examples of informative and instructional writing; it is now time to practise this kind of writing for yourself. Before doing so, read through the advice given below.

Being able to express instructions clearly and concisely in written English is an important skill to have. There are several key points that you, as the writer, should keep in mind. These are:

- You must have a thorough understanding and knowledge of the information that you want to pass on to the reader.

- However, do not make assumptions about your reader or expect him or her to know anything at all about the subject you are going to write about.
- When writing to inform, remember that the information you are giving is the most important feature; it is, therefore, advisable to adopt an impersonal, objective tone and not to distract your reader from the content of what you are saying by including too many imaginative and individual expressions. The style you use must be appropriate to the subject matter.
- Any devices you use to help make the information you are giving clearer to the reader (such as similes and metaphors) must be carefully considered to make sure that they do not suggest ideas that may lead to the reader being confused.
- Make sure that you are clear about the order in which you are going to make your points before you begin to write. Making notes and a rough draft will be greatly to your advantage.

Now let's look at an example of someone trying to give information through directions.

> 'Excuse me; I am a total stranger in this town and am looking for the bus station. Can you give me directions of how to get there, please?'
>
> 'Of course. I have lived here all my life so I know exactly where it is. I see that you are walking. Now, if you had a car, you would have to turn round and go back the way you came and then take the first road on the left because there is a one-way street coming up; however, that doesn't affect you if you are on foot. Now, the bus station is in Garden Square. That is about half a mile from here if you take the most direct route but you need to be careful as there are a couple of busy main roads you have to cross before you get there. So, you should keep walking up this road and then turn into Acacia Avenue; that isn't far, it's about the second or third turning. Anyway, carry on along Acacia Avenue for a bit and you will come to Laburnum Lane. Now you could go down here and take a short cut through the playing fields but you might get lost so I shouldn't do that. I would, because I live in Laburnum Lane and know where I am going but you would most probably get lost. So, carry on a bit farther after you have passed Laburnum Lane and then you will come to another street on your right – I'm not sure of its name, in fact, I don't think it has a street name sign on it, but you will recognise it because it's just before you get to the library which is down the next street. So carry on down this road – it isn't very long – and when you get to the end you will see the bus station just across the road on your right.'

How successful do you think this piece of direction giving is? Talk it over with a partner and make a list of all the things that are wrong with it. You could try to draw a map to illustrate the route but it will not be easy; for one thing, you would very soon be unsure as to whether you should turn left or right!

Exercise 4

(This and the following practice exercises are intended to help you to develop your skills in giving information clearly and succinctly in written

English. They are not typical of questions found in the Writing Paper of the Cambridge O Level English Language examination.)

Using the directions above as a rough guide, plan your own route to the bus station and then write it out as clearly and concisely as you can, remembering that the person for whom you are writing has never been to this town before.

Further practice exercises

Here are some more informative writing tasks to practise.

1. A friend wants to take up a sport or hobby with which you are very familiar. Give some information to your friend about what equipment he or she will need, where it can be obtained and approximately how much it will cost to get started on the activity.
2. Give instructions to a younger brother or sister about how to play a board game or a computer game.
3. Describe to one of your grandparents how a cell phone works and what features make it different from an ordinary telephone.
4. Give information to a new student in your school about the most important rules and policies.
5. Write instructions for a friend telling him or her how to prepare and cook your favourite food.

Tips for informative writing

In order to produce a good piece of informative or instructional writing, it is necessary to remember the following:

- **Vocabulary:** Your vocabulary should be precise and formal; try to keep the words you use as uncomplicated as you can without losing clarity of meaning. Remember: the content of what you are writing is the main issue.
- **Structure:** What you write should be clearly and logically structured through well-linked paragraphs. With some forms of informative or instructional writing it may even be more appropriate to use a series of clearly focused bullet points.
- **Accuracy of expression:** What you write should be in clearly demarcated sentences. When you are writing to give information it is best not to let your sentence structure become too long or involved. Remember that you are primarily concerned with conveying ideas in a coherent manner; short, unambiguous sentences are the most effective way of doing this.

Technical skills

Writing in sentences

- A sentence is a group of words making a complete unit of sense; it contains a **finite verb** (a verb that has a subject and shows tense). All sentences contain at least one **main clause** (a group of words containing a finite verb that can stand alone as a sentence). For example, 'You turn left at the crossroads.' A sentence that contains just one statement like this one is called a **simple sentence**. Some sentences, however, consist of two main ideas, joined by a **conjunction** (a word such as 'and' that links together two parts of a sentence). For example, 'You turn left at the crossroads and then carry on for another 100 metres.' This type of sentence is known as a **compound sentence**. Finally, some sentences contain a mixture of main and **subordinate clauses** (a clause, beginning with a conjunction plus a subject, or a relative pronoun that is dependent on a main clause for its meaning to be clear). For example, 'You carry on down for another 100 metres *when* you will find a signpost directing you to the bus station *which* is in Garden Square facing the post office.' This is known as a **complex sentence**.

- The end of a sentence is indicated by a **full stop**. For example, 'You turn left at the crossroads. The crossroads are very busy so you should watch the traffic carefully.' There are two distinct statements made in this piece of writing: each has a different subject and each contains a main clause with a finite verb. The only punctuation that has sufficient force to separate two such distinct statements is a full stop. One of the most common errors made by students in their writing is to use a comma to separate sentences when a full stop must be used.
- Most skilful writers will use a mixture of all three sentence types in their work and it is important to show that you, too, can confidently vary your sentence structures. However, remember that complex sentences are most effective for conveying involved and complicated ideas. When you are writing something that is intended to convey straightforward information or instructions, it is best not to over-complicate your sentence structures.

Paragraphs

- Whatever type of writing you are producing, it is important that you pay careful attention to your use of paragraphs as these will provide the backbone or structure which is necessary to make what you say clearly understood by the reader.
- A paragraph is a collection of sentences, all related to the same point, in which one idea is explored and developed.
- In factual writing each paragraph should contain a **topic sentence** that expresses the main point of the paragraph; the rest of the paragraph should develop and expand on this idea. The topic sentence can come at any point in a paragraph, depending on the effect you want to achieve.
- Each paragraph should develop from the one preceding it and link naturally into the one that follows, so that your writing shows a logical progression from one point to the next. Paragraph-linking devices will be looked at in more detail in Chapter 4 (see page 62).
- When planning a piece of informative or instructional writing, it is a good idea to do so by making your main instructions or pieces of information into the topic sentences which will underlie your paragraphs. You should then organise the paragraphs into the most logical order before you add the detail to produce your final draft.

Punctuation and sentence exercises

1 Rewrite the following, inserting full stops as necessary.
   a The teacher walked quietly into the room the boy at the front of the room did not notice and continued with his imitation of the teacher's way of speaking the rest of the class went silent
   b I really think that it is a good idea to read the instruction booklet on how to wire up this piece of electrical equipment before you turn it on you might have a nasty accident if you don't do so
   c This is the fastest car in its price bracket that you can buy it accelerates from 0 to 60 in five seconds you will find it very exciting to drive
   d A holiday in the Caribbean will give you the experience of a lifetime the beaches are fantastic you will meet the friendliest people on earth the food is delicious and original
   e My grandmother was a very happy woman she lived in the country all her life she never had very much money she lived a simple life her garden and small farm provided her with all the food she needed

2 Turn each of the following groups of simple sentences into one **complex** sentence using any method you think suitable.
   a Sarah was feeling bored. She had been on holiday for three days. It had been raining all week. She decided that she must get out of the house.
   b Sarah picked up the telephone. She dialled the number of her friend, Jane. Jane answered in a sleepy and tired voice.
   c Jane was pleased when she heard Sarah's voice. She had been very depressed by the bad weather. Now there might be a chance to do something interesting.
   d Sarah suggested that they went into town. Her older brother was at home. She would ask him if he would drive them in his car. They would call for Jane in 30 minutes.
   e Jane put down the telephone. She was very pleased with Sarah's suggestion. She ran into her bedroom. She needed to get ready quickly. She also wanted to eat some breakfast.

Paragraph exercise

Here are five topic sentences. Use each of them as the basis for a single paragraph of your own. Remember that all the ideas in each paragraph must relate to the topic sentence. You should try to vary the position of the topic sentences so that not all of them are used at the beginning of a paragraph.

a He mounted his bicycle and rode quickly away.
b These are the reasons why I particularly enjoy visiting my grandmother.
c It had been raining heavily without stopping for five days.
d The headteacher sat back in his comfortable chair and thought that the day had turned out better than he had feared.
e These are the main reasons why -------- is my favourite movie star. (*Fill in the blank with your favourite star's name.*)

3 NON-FICTION: DESCRIPTIVE TEXTS

Reading descriptive texts

Reading descriptions is all about taking in the detail. Perhaps nothing much happens in the paragraph but the writer has lingered on the view, or the person he is talking to, and added details to enable the reader to visualise what the view or the person looks like. The hills in the distance and the river winding through the fields appear in your mind's eye, or the wrinkles on the face of the elderly woman and the colour of her eyes. As a reader, your attention is held, as you can imagine what it would have been like to be there looking at that view or talking to that woman, and you become more engaged in what the writer is wanting to say.

Often it is not just the immediate picture that the writer wants the reader to imagine. When you look at something you also have a feeling about it: it pleases you or frightens you or reminds you of something else. When you read a description you should be aware of the feelings it evokes in you. Does the view sound pleasant and inviting, or threatening? Does the woman seem friendly or bad-tempered? You need knowledge of a wide vocabulary and of the contexts in which words are usually used so that you catch the subtleties. Later in this chapter we will talk in more detail about the techniques of writing descriptions, which will also help you recognise them in your reading. Many descriptions also include similes and metaphors to add details; those too are discussed later.

In a longer passage there is often one more dimension to consider, and that is the overall impression built up by the end. Take that view of the hills again; the first mention may be from the distance, misty, a long way off, the river in front, a desire to reach them. Next is perhaps from halfway there; the details of shape and size are clearer, you can pick out the cleft in the rocks you are making for; the river is swifter and the anticipation is greater. Finally, you arrive at the base of the waterfall in all its glory and are mesmerised by the sound of the water. The reader should have noticed not only the progression in the geographical details but also the accumulation of the effort taken to get there and the satisfaction of the arrival.

That progression is not usually as obvious as getting physically closer to a hill, but a good description always leads the reader to some feeling or to some awareness that the writer intends. When you are responding to a piece of descriptive writing in class or in an examination, remember to look back over the whole piece, not just for the pictorial details but also for the words and phrases in which the writer suggests the atmosphere and how you should be reacting by the end.

Non-fiction texts are concerned with giving true accounts of an event or an experience without any imaginary content. There are many forms of non-fiction, including biographies, autobiographies, travel writing, travel guides and academic textbooks, especially for subjects like History.

Here are three examples of non-fiction writing. Each of these pieces of writing gives us some information. However, they do so in different ways and for different purposes.

Passage 1 is aimed specifically at readers who are considering an adventurous trip to the River Amazon. It contains information about travel to many of the countries through which the Amazon flows, with details of what can be found in them and advice as to how travellers can make the most of their visit. This article originally appeared in the travel section of a newspaper and the information it contains is given in an informal tone, with the reader being addressed directly through the use of the **second person** pronoun 'you'.

Passage 2 is a historical account of the earthquake that destroyed Port Royal in Jamaica in 1692. This contains a lot of factual details about what happened on that day and it is written in the **third person**. However, it is also written as a narrative account and leads us into the story by focusing on a particular individual (Dr Emmanuel Heath) who was directly involved in the tragedy. This is another way in which the reader is engaged and interested in the information included in the passage.

Passage 3 is autobiographical in intention and consists of the writer's reminiscences about her childhood growing up in an area of Singapore; it is written in the **first person** but describes childhood experiences through the eyes of an adult whose life and character have been shaped by the experiences she is describing. The reader is, therefore, able to appreciate the details the writer gives from a dual perspective – that of the child whose life is being described and that of the adult who is describing the experiences and reflecting on them.

Read through all of these passages closely and then answer the questions that follow each of them.

Passage 1

The Amazon: Trip of a Lifetime

In the latest of our series on ultimate journeys, Chris Moss tells you how to tackle the Amazon

By Chris Moss

1:19PM GMT 01 Nov 2012

The Amazon is a 4,400-mile river with thousands of tributaries. It is a 2,600,000-square mile basin, draining rivers and streams in eight countries (Brazil, Bolivia, Peru, Ecuador, Colombia, Venezuela, Guyana and Suriname), as well as French Guiana. Its broadleaved forest is the largest on the planet and its biome – the forest combined with the savannah, floodplains and rivers – is a region of immense diversity, sheltering more than 30,000 plant species, 1,800 fish, 1,300 bird species, 311 mammals and 165 types of amphibian.

The superlatives state the facts, but the Amazon is clearly not a straightforward destination. For one thing, the main Amazon river flows through Brazil, Colombia and Peru, changing character as it changes its name; it's Amazonas in Spanish and Portuguese, but the upriver section in Brazil is called the Solimões and after it passes the tributary of Uy acali in Peru, it is known as the Marañón. All other rivers are tributaries. These three countries, along with Ecuador, where the Pastaza, Putumayo, Napo and Tigre drain into the Amazon, are the most obvious choices for a holiday, but all present different kinds of experiences and their own logistical challenges.

Brazil offers, arguably, the archetypal Amazon trip – a cruise from Belém on the Atlantic to Manaus or up to the Colombian border – but the interest here is more human or anthropological. You'll doubtless dance samba on deck at sunset, but you won't see many toucans.

Peru, Ecuador and, to a lesser extent, Colombia are notable for their wildlife. Where deforestation and industrialisation have devastated great expanses of the low-lying Brazilian Amazon, the headwaters are in better shape. For birders and lepidopterists, the banks of the tributaries and the forested slopes of the Andes provide plenty of entertainment. For those who want more specialist wildlife, tour companies take groups in search of spectacled bears, jaguars and rare monkeys.

Wherever you go, you will want to get away from the widest sections of the river. In fast tributaries, whitewater rafting and kayaking are options, but it is in the slower watercourses that wonders await. Small, quiet groups can be paddled or punted into channels to see capybara on the banks and capuchin monkeys in the canopy and, come nightfall, caiman, snakes and tree frogs.

When to travel

Given such a vast area, it is impossible to talk of a single weather system or neatly defined seasons. In the broadest terms, the rainy season in the Amazon is November or December to June (though Ecuador has a dry season between January and March). The river rises and floods the low-lying forests (called várzeas in Brazil) that lie along the banks, after which many channels become passable.

The dry – or drier – season, runs from July to December. As the temperature rises the mosquito numbers go down, and the receding rains expose trails and beaches. This can be good for hiking and fishing and for sightings of caiman as they compete for dwindling food sources.

How to travel

There are hundreds of ways into the Amazon. Independent travel is possible and may suit those with weeks to spare, but it comes with complications. You can fly into Belém and book onto a local boat and then arrange flights or epic bus journeys on from Manaus, or head directly for Iquitos or Leticia with only flights. You can also email the lodges in major parks such as the Tambopata, Manú or Yasuní reserves and the smarter boat operators (Delfin, Amazon Clipper, Manatee Amazon Explorer) directly and they will advise on logistics.

But you also need local operators for transfers and – because the best trips tend to be in remote areas – food, drink, water, boats and local guides (who may speak only Spanish or even an indigenous language, meaning a second guide).

➜

Sudden, torrential showers are daily occurrences across the Amazon, and flights are often delayed, and connections easily missed. In short, if you have limited time and want to go deep into the jungle or explore the backwaters, you're probably best organising your trip beforehand. Booking with a UK operator gives you a chance to browse what's on offer, as well as the security of insurance and backup.

The first question to ask is: land or water? Almost all visitors take to the river at some point but there's a huge difference between a four-day cruise and a three-hour transfer by motorised dugout. The second is: luxury or budget? The former will cut you off from local culture, but the latter may mean basic WCs, windowless chalets and warm soft drinks with dinner. A good ecolodge is often the best compromise and specialist tour operators will have surveyed the options and visited many of them.

Tactics by country

Brazil

Over the past two decades, the Pantanal wetlands in southern Brazil have replaced the Amazon as the wildlife destination par excellence. The country's vast Amazonian region, however, is still a popular choice for long voyages, whether on a cruise ship or a traditional riverboat.

Holland America, Princess, P & O and Silversea, among others, offer cruises that start in Brazil, Europe or the United States. But for the budget-conscious and anyone who wants to meet ordinary people, riverboats carrying passengers in hammocks (with a few air-conditioned cabins) depart every day from Belém to Manaus (stopping at Parintins, Santarém, and Monte Alegre), with connections on to Iquitos in Peru. These are cheap, basic and slow – book through a UK tour operator (visit lata.org for a list of firms specialising in Latin America).

Once upstream, the most popular options for wildlife watching are a cruise on small, smart riverboats from Manaus up the Rio Negro or to head farther upriver to Tefé to stay at the lovely Uakari floating lodge.

Brazilian highlights include the Manaus Opera House, pink dolphins, piranha fishing, the Rio Negro's anavilhanas (freshwater archipelago), caiman-spotting at night, Victoria amazonica waterlilies, flooded forests, pink-faced uakari monkeys and tarantulas.

Peru

The city of Iquitos – still not connected by road to most of Peru – remains the major hub for excursions into the Peruvian Amazon proper. From here visitors can either go by boat up to the Pacaya Samiria National Reserve, Peru's largest, or take the Nanay river to the Allpahuayo Mishana National Reserve. It is also possible to link up with Manaus on a local riverboat or, at the other extreme, on the luxurious SeaDream yacht.

In the last decade the Manú National Park, accessed via road from Cusco, and the Tambopata reserve near Puerto Maldonado, have become increasingly popular. They are part of the Madre de Dios river system and as well as great wildlife, ever-improving lodges and some intrepid options for kayaking, both are easy to combine with a Machu Picchu trip. Peru has a third Amazon region around Chachapoyas where the emphasis is on fine indigenous ruins (at Kuelap) and mummies (Leymebamba).

Peruvian highlights are Iquitos and its Casa de Fierro by Eiffel, strangling fig trees, canoeing in Lago Sandoval, river otter, cock of the rock, macaw and the parrot clay lick of Tambopata.

Ecuador

The headwaters of the Amazon in Ecuador are widely recognised as the site of some of the greatest biodiversity on Earth. The government is still contemplating exploiting the oil reserves in the Yasuní region but, for now at least, tourism provides a counterweight to the economic pressures.

Indigenous tribes such as the Huaorani and the Shuar and the more integrated Quechua communities accommodate visitors at basic lodges along the banks of several tributaries. Lodges are often isolated and getting to one may involve a flight – while boat trips are special, a small plane offers the best vantage point for seeing the full grandeur of the canopy.

Highlights include the indigenous tribes, ceibo trees, Huaorani Ecolodge and campsite, hummingbirds, blue morpho butterflies, the Yasuní Biosphere Reserve.

Colombia

Wildlife tourism is in its infancy in Colombia, but the Parque Nacional Amacayacu, accessed via Leticia, has – during the rainy season – flooded forests to rival any in Brazil and lower visitor numbers mean spottings of monkeys, river dolphins and the 468 bird species that live there are more likely. Visit parquesnacionales.gov.co for information (in Spanish only).

Where dozens of tour operators offer trips to the other Amazon countries, with Colombia you're best talking to a specialist such as Quartz Travel (01904 411188; quartz-travel.co.uk) or Colombia Holidays/Verdant Adventures (01603 340404; colombiaholidays.com) or intrepid companies such as Travel the Unknown (020 7183 6371; traveltheunknown.com) or World Odyssey (01905 731373; world-odyssey.com).

Colombian highlights include Leticia, Isla de los Micos, Puerto Nariño and mata-mata freshwater turtles.

Exercise 1

1 Make two lists. The first should contain all the geographical facts about the Amazon that are contained in the article. The second should include all the advice that the writer gives to people who might want to travel to the area. Try to divide the points in this second list into those that are facts and those which are the writer's opinions.

2 Your uncle and aunt who are middle-aged and very active are interested in visiting the Amazon. Write a letter to them explaining what the area has to offer tourists and suggesting which countries they would most benefit from visiting and why.

Passage 2

1692: Earthquake of Port Royal

'There never happens an earthquake,
but God speaks to men on Earth.'

Boston Puritan Cotton Mather, 1706

ON JUNE 7, 1692, after winding up his morning prayer service, Dr. Emmanuel Heath, the Anglican rector in Port Royal, left St. Paul's Church and walked to a nearby tavern. There he met his friend John White, who was president of the island's Council, and the two men got to chatting. Soon goblets of wormwood wine were brought out and White lit his customary pipe of tobacco. Before it was finished and the wine drunk, the floor suddenly began to rumble and shake. 'Lord, Sir,' the Rev. Heath asked his friend, 'what's this?'

Three hundred and nine years ago on this day, somewhere between 11:15 a.m. and noon (reports differ as to the actual time, although in the 1950s, in an archaeological first, divers are said to have found a watch which X-ray photography revealed to have stopped at 11.43 a.m.), the ground opened up in different places simultaneously, swallowing bodies and buildings alike.

Dead bodies and bones from uprooted graves covered the harbour, replacing ships tossed by the mammoth waves into the town's destroyed buildings and onto the shells of its once bustling streets. In total, between 1,500 and 2,000 people lost their lives.

Naval, merchant and fishing fleets were wrecked and the former jewel in England's 17th century colonies was brought to its knees. The duration of the quake is unclear; many Port Royal residents are documented as saying that it lasted at least 15 minutes, but most reports indicated that the catastrophe took no more than two to three minutes. That was all that was necessary to wipe out almost one-third of Port Royal's population, as in addition to those who died, up to 3,000 were reported to have sustained serious injuries.

Remarkably, both Heath and White survived this utter devastation. Rev. Heath is even believed to have reached his house and found everything in the same order in which he had left it. Many, including Rev. Heath, felt the quake to be a sign of divine retribution for Port Royal's reputation as the 'wickedest city in the world'.

Founded in 1650, Port Royal was first captured by the English in 1655 and turned into a strategic military and naval base. Initially intended as a heavily fortified garrison, by the late 17th century, the town had developed into the most important commercial centre in the English colonies. Port Royal's location in the middle of the Caribbean made it ideal for trade. Its location was also strategic for pillage and plunder as the many pirates who desired to launch attacks on the Spanish Main flocked to it. From 1660 to 1692, Port Royal became a haven for rogues such as the Welshman, Henry Morgan, and 'three-fingered' Jack Rackham.

According to a September 2000 'History Today' article by Larry Gragg, Port Royal was densely populated, covering little more than 50 acres. It was filled with close to 6,500 people of various professions – 'Smiths, Carpenters, Bricklayers, Joyners, Turners, Cabinet Makers, Tanners, Shoemakers, Taylors, Hatters, Upholsters, Ropemakers, Glasiers, Painters, Carvers, Armourers, and Combmakers.' They lived in nearly 2,000 multi-storey, often brick, buildings that miraculously managed to stand upon a foundation of sand. There were many places of worship for Roman Catholics, Presbyterians, Baptists, Quakers and Jews.

Historical accounts reveal that close on the heels of the earthquake and during its many aftershocks, looters broke into homes and warehouses taking every thing of value. The dead were said to have been robbed of all they had on them, and on the very night of the quake, many in the destroyed town were even said to have been back at their 'old trades of swearing and rioting'.

The Rev. Heath hoped that this terrible judgment would stand as a warning and that God would make these people of ill repute reform their lives. Some, like Boston-based Puritan minister, Cotton Mather, believed God intended it as a warning to Christians everywhere.

If it was such, it went unheeded. All that was left of Port Royal was about 25 acres, a substantially depleted population and a skeleton of a town. Yet, five years later a visitor to Jamaica described Port Royal as a place where the residents 'regard nothing but money, and value not how they get it'.

Although it continued to serve as a British naval base throughout the 18th century, Port Royal yielded its commercial role to its neighbour across the harbour, Kingston. A fire in 1703 and a devastating hurricane in 1722 hastened Port Royal's full decline. By 1774, there were scarcely a hundred houses in Port Royal.

Exercise 2

Imagine you are Dr Emmanuel Heath. It is now 1710 and you are writing your personal account of the earthquake. Include in your account:

- details of the earthquake itself and its aftermath
- how other people behaved
- your thoughts and feelings about the earthquake and what you think Port Royal will be like in the future.

You should use only details from the passage. Write using your own words as far as possible.

Read Passage 3 and answer the questions after each section.

Passage 3

Growing Up in Katong

Cynthia Wee-Hoefer reminisces on growing up in a particular area of Singapore during the 50s and 60s of the last century.

It was a rather dusty lane, leading to the original Marine Parade, a seaside promenade, on one end, and to the main East Coast Road on the other. This is where I grew up, and I recall a childhood 5 swirling with the language, habits and culture of the Peranakans who lived alongside the Eurasians, China-born Chinese, Boyanese Malays, Jews and an exotic parade of Indians of all castes and colours. This was Singapore at the end of British rule and the 10 dawn of independence.

I grew up in a lane off East Coast Road which was affectionately known to Katongites and trishaw riders as Longkang Besar. While it is true that a large open drain channelled the flow of water and debris from 15 the inland to the sea at Marine Parade, it always baffled me why others referred to it as Jacob's Lane. It was only recently that a former resident, Eddy, revealed that a tall, dark and skinny Eurasian named Jacob lived there. There was no street sign to say that 20 it was East Coast Road, but the houses numbered 150A to 150P indicated the location of 16 terraced houses to the postman. The lane was obscure, tucked between a row of double-storeyed shophouses and elegant setback terraced residences on the main road. When giving instructions to friends and taxi drivers, 25 I had to say that it was 'after the Joo Chiat traffic lights, the small lane on the right, opposite the Shell station.'

Our beloved Sandy Lane was flanked by neat rows of raised terrace houses with curlicue frescoed 30 fronts, patterned mosaic steps and a narrow veranda. The houses were pretty and deep to accommodate three bedrooms, a living room, a dining room, and a kitchen covered by a zinc roof. There was a toilet (originally of the bucket system but modernised years 35 later), a bathroom, and an airy basement that worked as an additional storage space, sleeping quarter and hide-and-seek playground. Our courtyard was enclosed by high walls which separated us from the neighbours, but the noises still penetrated across, 40 providing lots of juicy details especially when family quarrels exploded. They don't build houses like these anymore.

Exercise 3

1. Draw a sketch map to show the area described by the writer. Mark on it the sea and Marine Parade, East Coast Road and the lane, and add as many of the buildings mentioned as you can. Is the description detailed enough to make this an easy task?
2. How many different names for the lane are there in the passage? Why do you think the writer uses them all?
3. What does the word 'swirling' (line 5) suggest about the neighbourhood?
4. The writer says that the lane was 'obscure' (line 22). What fact does she give to back up this opinion?
5. Give the meaning of the following words as used in the passage:
   - a tucked between (lines 22–3)
   - b accommodate (line 32)
   - c juicy (line 41)

We were surrounded by greenery and nature. From
45 the entrance we faced a mature frangipani tree (which
we turned into a tree house) and fruiting guavas,
while rows of spider lilies and periwinkles bordered
the drain. Giant tamarind and flame of the forest trees
provided shade. We were never short of asam or biji
50 sagar seeds for our five-stone games.

The boys had an unlimited supply of fighter spiders
which were stored in matchboxes with a single
leaf for food and spittle for drink. The moths and
insects attracted to the lights at night were caught
55 and shown off and later released. My favourite was
an insect which had a hard shell at its thorax. When
pressed against the matchbox or tin case, its head
would instinctively knock the surface several times,
which made a great game where we had to guess
60 the number of times the insect would knock against
the box.

The lane was always potholed in areas and a bane for
the poor trishaw rider or the hawker with his tricycle.
On rainy days, we had to tread carefully over the
65 puddles and woe to the newcomer at night, who with
one wrong step could end up with soaked feet and
trouser cuffs.

We caught tadpoles after the rainy days which we
took to school for our science class. During the dry
season, we had to sprinkle water from a tin can to 70
keep the dust down. Resourceful as we children
were, we found endless use for the bare ground.
With strokes of a stick, we would create hopscotch
diagrams, circle games, start and finish lines for our
endless races along the traffic-free lane. Naturally, we 75
dug up holes for bolah lasing, a game whereby one
player rolled a tennis ball towards an arrangement of
holes in the ground. And if it lopped into your hole,
you had to grab the ball and try to hit any one of the
players. If you failed, you were penalised by standing 80
on one spot with your back facing the rest of the
party while someone got to hit you, the target, with
the tennis ball. Whatever game caught our fancy –
marbles, hide-and-seek, rounders – it was almost
always played en masse with the neighbourhood 85
children, and outdoors in the late afternoon when the
sun was about to set.

Exercise 4

6 From the first two paragraphs in this section, find five words or phrases that suggest the abundance of the surrounding nature.

7 Why do you think the writer's favourite insect was the one with the hard shell?

8 What does the writer imply about herself by her mention of 'woe to the newcomer' (line 65)?

9 Give the meaning of the following words as used in the passage:
   a bane (line 62)
   b resourceful (line 71)
   c en masse (line 85)

The best part of life in Katong was the casualness of dropping in at a friend's or relative's house. One 90 always visited with a small gift – a bag of rambutans from the garden or a bottle of pickles, and sometimes this was reciprocated with something or other from the larder. Such was the camaraderie.

Marine Parade was everybody's playground. Every 95 Sunday or public holiday, we children used to enjoy the festivities the park would hold. There was a weekly joget or dance in a bungalow house with a roomy veranda, next to the beach mansion of Tan Lark Sye (both now demolished). The air was heavily 100 scented with the fragrances of the day – Evening in Paris and bunga chempaka and jasmine in the ladies' coifed hair. The fashion of the day was the body-fitting baju and sarong ensemble that the Dutch-Indonesian singer Anneke Gronloh popularised. It was quite thrilling to stand on our toes to try and 105 get a view of the action.

The biggest event in Marine Parade when the area became totally packed with picnickers was the mandi safar, an act of ablution which was originally a Hindu practice. Families would arrive with pots of food, 110 seats and mats and a portable radio and party away with abandoned merriment dunking into the frothing sea and playing games. It was sheer delight to watch young and old, the well-off and the poor, put aside their daily grind for a day of pleasure. For the rest 115 of the community, the crowd added to their day of leisure as they tried to get a seat at the outdoor Teo's cafe which was a two-storey bungalow house where hawkers sold some of the best kueh pai tee, laksa, yong tau foo and satay on the island. 120

Exercise 5

10 What is the focus of each of the three sections? Explain how they build up to an overall picture of the writer's childhood in this area.

11 The writer found her childhood an enjoyable experience. By referring closely to the content of the passage and the language she uses to describe it, explain fully how she communicates this enjoyment to the reader.

Further reading exercises on descriptive texts

Read the passages below and then answer the questions that follow.

Passage 4

Onward Virgin sailors

Only three months after Steve Boggan and friends learnt to sail in Kent they chartered their own yacht in the Caribbean.

1 When my friend Jonathan told me that we were going to sail a yacht in the Caribbean within three months, I just laughed and ordered another drink at the bar. My maritime experience extended as far as an hour in a rowing boat in Colwyn Bay. 5

2 It was that kind of conversation; not so different from our plans to learn to fly or buy an entire village in southern Italy. Better than his scheme to set up a windsurfing school in Spain, worse than mine to buy a bar in Mexico. Basically, it was a bar plan. 10

3 Now several weeks later, I deeply regretted those drinks and that bar. Lashed by sleet on the milk-chocolate waters of the Medway estuary, in the South-East corner of England, I was frozen, seasick and desperately unimpressed by the view. 15 Everywhere I looked, on either bank or beyond stinking mud flats, were power stations belching steam into grey, lowering skies. I'd kill him for this. The only thing that kept me going was the hope that we would soon be doing this in the sub-tropical 20 waters of the British Virgin Islands – or the BVIs, as they are known to yachting enthusiasts.

4 Jonathan was a keen windsurfer but he had no sailing experience. He simply wanted a bigger piece of plastic beneath his feet. With that in mind, 25 he had persuaded me, my partner Suzanne, his wife Michele and our friend Deborah to undertake 'competent crew' courses approved by the Royal Yachting Association while he added a 'day skipper' course on top. 30

5 The competent crew course was over three weekends and cost £550 each. Jonathan's skipper's course comprised nine days – four in the classroom, five on a boat – and included tuition in navigation, radio operation and practical sailing, and came to an extra 35 £780. You eat on board, sleep on board, come close to hypothermia on board and learn to sail while being shouted at by beefy and very experienced instructors. But don't be put off – they only shout at you because (a) you are very stupid and you must not 40 forget this, and (b) they must be sure that you hear every order they give or you might screw things up. And that could be dangerous for all concerned.

6 Sailing at a basic level is not easy but neither is it rocket science. We were taught the principles – 45

➜

basically, how sails use lift in a similar way to the wings of an aeroplane, enabling you to travel into (actually, just off) the wind. We learned the ropes – actually called 'sheets' – and how to use the sails. We practised tacking into the wind and gybing with it at our backs and became proficient in tying up to buoys and jetties, anchoring, tying knots ...

7 Now all we had to do was persuade someone to hire a £200,000 yacht for as little money as possible to a group of people with virtually no experience. I don't know whether this is good or rather worrying news for your readers, but we had hardly any trouble at all doing so.

8 We found the charming Windward Islands Cruising company in London, fully described our concerns about our inexperience and let them get on with it. In no time at all, they had secured us a three-cabin Beneteau Oceanis 393 yacht (just under 40ft long) at £2,675 for 12 days.

9 In retrospect, the ease with which we chartered a boat probably had something to do with our destination. The BVIs form part of an archipelago rubbing up against the US Virgin Islands some 80 miles east of Puerto Rico. They comprise around 50 islands and islets set in unfeasibly clear water and nestle up closely to one another. So you're never out of sight of dry land and there are no strong tides, which makes them very attractive for novice sailors. Every instructor we asked for advice told us this was the best place for people of our limited experience. With our newly acquired skills we would, they said, be perfectly safe.

10 We flew to Antigua, hopped on the flight to Tortola and slept overnight on our yacht, *Bellezza*, at anchor in Hodges Creek. The next day, a skipper accompanied us to familiarise us with the vessel. And then we were alone, unsupervised and not a little apprehensive.

11 We had decided to take in the islands of Tortola, Virgin Gorda, Cooper Island, Jost Van Dyke, Marina Cay and whatever others took our fancy as we sailed around on *Bellezza*. We were beginning to feel very grand and were no longer putting things in the kitchen; we were 'stowing' them in 'the galley'.

12 Naturally, each island is different but they are similar in character; hilly, covered in scrub, surrounded by coral reefs to some extent or other, and blessed by lots and lots of sandy white beaches, many sheltered by coconut palms. You can go round them in an orderly fashion, but we opted to go around the houses so that we could get as much sailing experience as possible.

13 After a night moored in Trellis Bay off Beef Island, where we ate fabulously at The Last Resort, we headed off for Jost Van Dyke, stopping for the afternoon at a cartoon strip island called Sandy Spit, which is smaller than a football pitch and boasts one palm tree.

14 Jost Van Dyke has several restaurants and bars in Great Harbor, most famously Foxy's, which is described as being 'wild' in various American guidebooks. Here we had our first taste of the islands' trademark cocktail, made from pineapple and orange juices, and cream of coconut.

15 There were some things we had to get used to, however. Needless to say, we found that most places require you to radio ahead for a dinner booking which can sometimes be as early as 6.45pm. You will often find no food available after 8pm and you may find yourself in darkness by 10pm. Many of the islands have nowhere to buy provisions, take on water or buy fuel, so you have to plan carefully; ie always have your own food and drink in the fridge.

16 But what did we care? We were here for the sailing! We ticked off all the islands we wanted to see, some with a flying visit and a lie down on the beach or a snorkel with turtles and stingrays. On others we stayed longer for one or two nights, often depending on how good the local restaurant was. There was rarely more than one. 125

17 Reputedly, the food in the BVIs is not very good and we had mixed experiences. True, in parts there is too much of an American influence and a profusion of burgers and fries. But, in fairness, the American-imported beef is fabulous. Seafood, 130 however, can be somewhat hit or miss.

18 Davide Pugliese, the chef who served up our best meal at the excellent Brandywine Bay restaurant on Tortola, warns that tropical fish poisoning, or ciguatera, can be got from predatory fish caught 135 around local reefs. These include barracuda, grouper, snapper, parrot fish and puffer fish. As a result, he imports his. Elsewhere, be careful.

19 Sailing your own vessel gives you an enormous amount of freedom but there are also limitations – 140 the accommodation can be cramped and you are not always in control of your own destiny. Each day sees a mad rush to tie up to a buoy before they are all taken, or endure the worry inherent in dropping your anchor: Will it hold? Will you be 145 swept out to sea or on to rocks? And for heavens sake, never drop it on coral!

20 Still, tying up by 3pm is a small inconvenience when you find you have to be in bed by 9pm anyway.

21 The rest of the time you are free to enjoy long, 150 languid days sailing between islands and landing your dinghy on deserted beaches.

22 Over 12 days, we changed. On the first, we pulled down our sails, put the engine on and ran from a bit of rough sea. By the last, we were flying along 155 and sailing instinctively. It was a long way from the power stations of the Medway – there was no doubt the training had paid off.

23 And, contrary to our worst nightmares, all we broke was a plate that fell from a cupboard one day while, 160 clinging to the deck, we sailed at an impossible angle in a fierce wind, yelling at one another and not quite believing that this really was us.

Exercise 6

1 In the first two paragraphs, the writer gives **three** reasons why at first he did not take seriously Jonathan's suggestion that they should go sailing in the Caribbean. What are they?
2 In the third paragraph, what is the writer implying about the waters of the Medway estuary by calling them 'milk-chocolate'? What other word in the paragraph reinforces this implication?
3 What else did the writer find unpleasant about his experiences on the training course in the Medway estuary? How does he put across the strength of his feelings? (*Hint*: how many of the senses does he include in his description?)
4 Why does the writer think it could be worrying that they had little difficulty in hiring a yacht in the Caribbean? (paragraph 7)
5 What **three** reasons are given in the passage for why the waters around the British Virgin Islands are suitable for inexperienced sailors? (paragraph 9) Use your own words as far as possible.
6 What tone is the writer using when he says, 'we were no longer putting things in the kitchen; we were "stowing" them in "the galley"'? (paragraph 11)

7 Explain in your own words the sort of route the writer and his companions took around the islands. What reason did he give for doing it in the way they did? (paragraph 12)
8 What is unusual about the fish cooked by the chef in the Brandywine Bay restaurant? (paragraph 18)
9 What does the passage imply is likely to happen if sailors drop anchor on coral? (paragraph 19)
10 What detail in the penultimate paragraph tells you that the writer and his companions had become fully confident in handling their boat?
11 What is the overall purpose of this article? Do you think it is successful? Give reasons for your answer.
12 Explain, using your own words, the meaning of the following words and phrases, as used in the passage:
- lashed (line 12)
- lowering (line 18)
- beefy (line 38)
- unfeasibly (line 70)
- apprehensive (line 83)
- profusion (line 129)
- hit or miss (line 131)
- predatory (line 135)
- inherent (line 144)
- languid (line 151)

Summarising task

a Make notes on **(i)** how the writer and his friends prepared for their sailing holiday and **(ii)** what they found enjoyable about their time in the British Virgin Islands.
b Now link your notes into a connected piece of writing, explaining **(i)** how the writer and his friends prepared and **(ii)** what they found enjoyable.

Here are two more examples of descriptive writing. Read them carefully and discuss with a partner which you find more effective and why.

Passage 5 describes the writer's experience as a young boy when he visited his somewhat eccentric grandfather who lived in a village in Wales.

Passage 5

In the middle of the night I woke from a dream full of whips and lariats as long as serpents, and runaway coaches and mountain passes, and wide, windy gallops over cactus fields, and I heard the old man in the next room crying, 'Gee-up!' and 'Whoa!' and trotting his tongue on the roof of his mouth.

It was the first time I had stayed in grandpa's house. The floorboards had squeaked like mice as I climbed into bed, and the mice between the walls had creaked like wood as though another visitor was walking on them. It was a mild summer night, but curtains had flapped and branches beaten against the window. I had pulled the sheets over my head, and soon was roaring and riding in a book.

'Whoa there, my beauties!' cried grandpa. His voice sounded very young and loud, and his tongue had powerful hooves, and he made his bedroom into a great meadow. I thought I would see if he was ill, or had set his bedclothes on fire, for my mother had said that he lit his pipe under the blankets, and had warned me to run to his help if I smelt smoke in the night. I went on tiptoe through the darkness to his bedroom door, brushing against the furniture and upsetting a candlestick with a thump. When I saw there was light in the room I felt frightened, and as I opened the door I heard grandpa shout, 'Gee-up!' as loudly as a bull with a megaphone.

He was sitting straight up in bed and rocking from side to side as though the bed were on a rough road and the knotted edges of the counterpane were his reins; his invisible horses stood in a shadow beyond the bedside candle. Over a white flannel nightshirt he was wearing a red waistcoat with walnut-sized brass buttons. The overfilled bowl of his pipe smouldered among his whiskers like a little, burning hayrick on a stick. At the sight of me, his hands dropped from the reins and lay blue and quiet, the bed stopped still on a level road, he muffled his tongue into silence, and the horses drew softly up.

'Is there anything the matter, grandpa?' I asked, though the clothes were not on fire. His face in the candlelight looked like a ragged quilt pinned upright on the black air and patched all over with goat-beards.

He stared at me mildly. Then he blew down his pipe, scattering the sparks and making a high, wet dog-whistle of the stem, and shouted: 'Ask no questions.'

After a pause, he said slyly: 'Do you ever have nightmares, boy?'

I said: 'No.'

'Oh, yes, you do,' he said.

I said I was woken by a voice that was shouting to horses.

'What did I tell you?' he said. 'You eat too much. Who ever heard of horses in a bedroom?'

He fumbled under his pillow, brought out a small tinkling bag, and carefully untied its strings. He put a sovereign in my hand, and said: 'Buy a cake.' I thanked him and wished him good night.

As I closed my bedroom door, I heard his voice crying loudly and gaily, 'Gee-up! Gee-up!' and the rocking of the travelling bed.

Dylan Thomas

In Passage 6 another writer describes visiting his grandparents who lived in a house in the south of England.

Passage 6

The house my grandparents lived in was nice and big. I used to visit them with my parents when I was a child. It had quite a large garden and there were some fruit trees in it. I remember that my father once climbed up into one of the trees to pick some plums. He fell out of the tree. He did not fall very far and did not hurt himself. My mother and grandparents laughed but I was worried and cried.

My grandparents had a lot of old furniture in their house. They had a large china vase which had a Chinese pattern on it. One day I was running in the house and knocked the vase off the table. It fell on to the floor and broke. My grandmother was very upset and my parents had to apologise for my behaviour. I was only about four years old and could not understand why people were upset. I thought that the vase could not have cost much money because it broke so easily.

We always visited my grandparents on Sunday afternoons. We used to walk to their house. It was quite a long way from where we lived and it took about thirty minutes to reach there. It was not a very interesting walk as it was from one side of the town to the other. However, the road in which my grandparents lived had some nice trees in it. My grandmother always made us a cup of tea when we arrived (although I did not like tea very much) and we always had toasted fruit teacakes with butter on them to eat.

My grandparents were a typical old couple. My grandmother was quite often bad-tempered. My grandfather had been in the Royal Marines and he always showed me his ceremonial sword which he kept brightly polished. When the Second World War started he was afraid that England would be invaded and so he buried many of the family's valuables in his garden so that they would not be looted. I understand that when the war finished he went to dig them up but could not remember exactly where he had buried them. I remember that he was quite often digging up bits of his garden trying to find them when we came to visit.

Sometimes, when my grandmother was in a bad mood, my grandfather used to shut himself away in his garden shed to escape from her. This made our visits a little difficult at times. Sadly, my grandfather died when I was quite young and my grandmother moved away to live with one of my uncles in a different part of the country. I never visited the house again.

Both of these passages describe childhood experiences. You probably found Passage 5 more interesting than Passage 6 and in your discussion probably decided that this was because the writer had used language more imaginatively and in a more lively way so that the boy's experience was much more immediate to the reader. Passage 6 contains details that could be made just as interesting as those in the first one but the language used lacks precision and interest.

Exercise 7

1 Choose a selection of descriptive details from Passage 5 and explain as fully as you can how they help you to share the boy's experience and to visualise clearly his grandfather.
2 Comment on the language used by the writer of Passage 6 and suggest ways in which the descriptions could be made more vivid, for example through the use of adjectives, similes and metaphors, and choice of verbs and adverbs.

Writing to describe

In Chapter 2 you practised writing to give factual information in an objective, formal way; this chapter has so far presented you with some examples of writing, the purpose of which is to describe places and experiences. In several of them the description is based on the writer's own experience and is written from a personal viewpoint. In these examples the writing is more complex than the examples used in Chapter 2 as in these passages, the writers have allowed themselves to express their opinions and feelings about what they are describing. This means that you, as the reader, have not only gained an awareness and understanding of what they are describing but have also gained an impression of the character of the writer. The description of the Port Royal earthquake, even though its main concern is to give information about what happened is, nevertheless, given a human focus as it allows us to understand the event through the medium of Dr Heath, and this provides an extra dimension to the account.

Descriptive writing tasks are likely to cover describing one of the following subjects:

- a place
- a scene
- a building or part of a building
- an event or an occasion such as a family celebration
- a person or an animal.

Here are some key points to remember when you are writing to describe:

- Always try to base what you are describing on your personal knowledge; you cannot give a clear picture of your subject to the reader unless you have a clear picture in your own mind. However, remember that you are in control of what you are writing and you can change and distort details deliberately to create a particular impression.
- You need to decide on your viewpoint before beginning to write. For example, are you going to write from a first-person angle or are you going to adopt a more general, impersonal approach? Whichever you choose, you should stay consistent throughout this piece of writing.

- How are you going to structure your description? For example, you could take a geographical approach and move round the scene from left to right, or from distant to close at hand; or a chronological approach by different times of the day; or you could work through the different senses of sight, hearing, touch, smell, taste. Whichever you choose, you should try to make the links between the different sections of your structure seem natural and not too mechanical.
- Be selective in what you write. If you try to include every little detail that comes into your mind there is a serious danger that you will overload the details and that your reader will become confused.
- As in all writing, keep your reader clearly in mind; you may know the person or place you are describing very well but it is unlikely that your reader will. It is important that you give some brief context in which to set your description.
- Although your main purpose is to give a clear impression of your subject matter to the reader, remember that it is likely to help make your writing more interesting if you come over as an interesting and reliable witness to it. Unlike the informative writing you did for the exercises in the previous chapter, when you are writing this type of description you should include your own opinions and feelings about whatever it is you are describing. However, you need not always convey these feelings directly; they can be expressed very effectively by the words you use.
- Be very careful to write in complete sentences and include enough verbs to keep your grammatical structure clear. When you are trying to add a small detail to another small detail to another small detail it is easy to lapse into adding phrase to phrase to phrase. The occasional non-sentence for emphasis can be effective, but if the whole description contains no verbs it just looks as if you do not know how to write.

Tips for descriptive writing

- **Adjectives** are words that qualify (or describe) a noun. They are, therefore, important tools for descriptive writing and should be chosen carefully. For example, you can convey different shades of meaning depending on the adjectives you use. To say, 'My grandfather is an *energetic*, *carefree* man' has quite a different meaning from saying, 'My grandfather is a *thoughtful*, *careful* man'. However, it is a good idea to use adjectives sparingly; using too many of them can have the effect of slowing down your writing.
- **Verbs** are words that express action or a state of being (for example, 'he *ran* very fast'; 'he *became* angry'). A verb is the most important word in a sentence and a well-chosen one can significantly increase the power of your description. For example, consider the different impressions given by the verbs in each of these sentences: The teacher *strode* into the room. The teacher *crept* into the room. The teacher *stormed* into the room. How many different ways can you think of expressing 'he said'?
- **Adverbs** are words that modify (or add to the meaning of) verbs and, again, are valuable tools in giving a precise description. Consider how these adverbs modify the sense in the sentences above: The teacher

strode *purposefully* into the room. The teacher crept *cautiously* into the room. The teacher stormed *furiously* into the room.

- **Similes** are comparisons in which one thing is said to be like another and are introduced by the words *like* or *as*. For example: Grandpa shouted as loudly *as a bull with a megaphone*; his pipe was *like a little burning hayrick on a stick*. Both of these descriptions make the scene more vivid and also add a slight touch of humour to the writing. Remember, if you use similes, there must be a clear point of comparison between the two parts of the description and it is important that the comparison does not undermine the effect you want to create. In a sentence like 'The garden was as peaceful as a graveyard', the comparison with a graveyard implies that the garden was a rather cold and deserted place which, judging from the pleasant word 'peaceful', is probably not the impression the writer wanted to give; the atmosphere has become confused. Remember also that it is important that you try to choose similes that are original and alive. Comparisons such as 'he ran like the wind' and 'the dog was as white as snow' have been used so much that they have lost any real vital force and mean no more than 'he ran very quickly' and 'the dog was very white'. Such tired comparisons are known as **clichés** and a good writer will try to avoid them at all costs.
- **Metaphors** are comparisons in which one thing is expressed in terms of another – in effect, a metaphor is a concentrated simile. They are also a good way of giving immediacy to your descriptive writing. For example, 'the rain came down *like a waterfall*' is a simile whereas 'the *waterfall of rain* washed away the soil' is a metaphor. In it the rain *becomes* a waterfall rather than the writer just saying it is like one and the readers immediately associate both ideas in their minds. As with using similes in your writing, it is important that you make sure that the metaphors you choose are original and have clear points of comparison.

Technical skills

Vocabulary: choosing the precise word – synonym

One of the key qualities of a successful writer is the ability to choose exactly the right word to convey precisely the meaning you wish to give. Precise vocabulary is important when you are writing to describe as it allows you to convey the exact sense of your subject rather than simply giving a general impression of it.

English is a language that has a very large vocabulary and contains many words to give exactly the right shade of meaning for what a writer intends to communicate. A word that has a similar meaning to another is known as a **synonym** and English is rich in these. However, very, very few words mean *exactly* the same as another one and it is the ability to distinguish the subtle differences in meaning between synonyms that is the sign of both a good writer and also a thoughtful reader. For example, here is a list of synonyms for the word 'sad':

bitter, despairing, despondent, disconsolate, dismal, distressed, doleful, down, downcast, despairing, heartbroken, low, pessimistic

Each one of these words has its own particular meaning and its own context in which it is used, and whether you use it correctly or not depends very much on the context of what you are writing. For example, if it's raining hard and you are unable to have a barbecue with your friends on the beach, you might describe your state of mind as being *downcast* but it would be over-dramatic to describe yourself as feeling *heartbroken* or *despairing.*

Synonym exercises

1 Choose ten words from the synonyms for *sad* and use each in a sentence, in order to bring out clearly its particular meaning. For example, *The sun had not shone all day; the sky was a dark, dirty grey and there was rain in the air; it was the most dismal day I have ever known.*
2 Use each of the following synonyms for *eat* in a sentence to bring out its meaning clearly: *dine, feast, munch, nibble, scoff.*
3 Write out the following description choosing **one** of each of the words in brackets in order to produce a consistent description:

The sea was (calm/relaxed) now although only an hour before it had been (savage/pitiless) in its violence. The storm had (raged/swept) throughout the island, uprooting (ancient/feeble) trees and threatening the (safety/comfort) of all the inhabitants. Even those who lived in (strongly built/secure) brick houses felt the force of the wind as it (ripped/tore) at their roofs. The unfortunate inhabitants of the (less stable/flimsy) buildings knew that it was unlikely that they would still have (homes/houses) on the following day.

Focusing on details

Another key point to remember when writing a description is to focus on details; for example, the writer of Passage 5 on pages 36–7 could easily have written *over a flannel nightshirt he was wearing a red waistcoat* without changing the overall sense of what he was saying; however, the addition of the details concerning the colour of the nightshirt (*white*) and the buttons on the waistcoat (*walnut-sized brass buttons*) makes the description come alive.

Punctuation: commas

Commas are important punctuation devices; however, it is easy to misuse them. The following are the main occasions when commas should be used; you will notice that six of these uses are purely mechanical, the other one requires a little more care.

- To separate words (especially adjectives) or phrases in a list or series (except for the last two words which are usually joined by 'and'). For example: 'Mr O'Grady was a mean, cruel, bad-tempered, miserly and thoroughly unpleasant man.'
- To mark off the name or title of a person being addressed. 'Mr O'Grady, you've just dropped your wallet.' or "Excuse me, Mr O'Grady, could you please give me my money back?'
- To mark off words or phrases in apposition (that is, words which are parallel in meaning to others in the same sentence). For example, 'Mr

O'Grady, the shopkeeper, is a very rich man', which tells the reader that Mr O'Grady is the shopkeeper and is a very rich man. Note the difference from 'Mr O'Grady, the shopkeeper is a very rich man', which is telling Mr O'Grady that the shopkeeper (who is someone else) is a very rich man.
- To mark off words and phrases such as *however, therefore, nevertheless, moreover, on the other hand*, etc. that have been added into a sentence. For example: 'Make sure, however, that when you are talking to Mr O'Grady, you are always polite.'
- To mark off clauses, or phrases beginning with a participle when it is necessary to make a pause in reading. For example: 'Seeing that my father was also a rich man, Mr O'Grady asked him if he would like a drink.' Note that if the clause or phrase is in the middle of the sentence as in 'Mr O'Grady, seeing that my father was also a rich man, asked him if he would like a drink', there should be a pair of commas, to mark the beginning and the end of the clause or phrase.
- In conjunction with speech marks to indicate the beginning of a passage of direct speech: 'Mr O'Grady rose to his feet and said, "......".'
- To separate an adjectival clause beginning with 'who', 'whom' or 'which' from the rest of the sentence, when it is **non-**defining. This is a particularly tricky use of the comma, and requires thought. In the sentence: 'Mr O'Grady ordered that all the schoolchildren who were in his shop should be punished', written without commas, the clause 'who were in his shop' tells the reader which children should be punished, that is it *defines* the group of children. But if written **with** commas as: 'Mr O'Grady ordered that all the schoolchildren, who were in his shop, should be punished', the clause *who were in his shop* is non-defining and, therefore, means that all the children in the school must be punished and they happened to be in his shop at that particular time. The meaning of the main sentence would be the same whether the clause was there or not.

There is, however, one over-riding rule about using commas, and that is that they should be helpful to the reader. Their use has the effect of breaking up a sentence into smaller parts, signalling a slight pause in reading and helping the reader to grasp the meaning. For example: 'Mr O'Grady, bad-tempered and angry, stormed into the school building, knocked on the Principal's door and then, before the Principal could ask him what he wanted, launched into a tirade about the bad behaviour of young people today.'

But consider this example:

> Mr O'Grady, however, the shopkeeper, bad-tempered, angry and rude, seeing the Principal's door was open, stormed in.

Those commas follow the fourth, third and first rules, but having so many so close together impedes the flow of the sentence rather than helps. It would be acceptable to write:

> Mr O'Grady however, the shopkeeper, bad-tempered angry and rude, seeing the Principal's door was open, stormed in.

Conversely, in a longer sentence it sometimes helps to put in a comma at a natural break when technically by the rules it is not necessary. This example is from the Virgin Islands passage you read earlier:

> 'Each day sees a mad rush to tie up to a buoy before they are all taken, or endure the worry inherent in dropping your anchor.'

A comma is not required by the rules before 'or', but without it the reader might run on 'before they are all taken or endure …' and lose the sense of the sentence. Inserting a comma clarifies where the break comes.

Finally, always remember that **complete sentences must always be closed with a full stop, never a comma.** If you cannot remember how to distinguish between the need for a comma and a full stop, look back at page 21.

Punctuation exercise

Rewrite the following passage, inserting commas and full stops as necessary.

> Mr Thompson the Principal of Happy Valley High School was not a happy man he had just received a communication from a very angry rich and powerful man named Mr O'Grady who wanted him Mr Thompson to punish a group of children who had been in Mr O'Grady's shop after school knowing that Mr O'Grady was the sort of person who would not listen to any excuses and who no matter how many times anyone tried to persuade him otherwise would never change his mind Mr Thompson nevertheless felt that he ought to try to put in a good word for the children in his school who were he knew not really naughty just high spirited reluctantly he opened his door to Mr O'Grady when he heard him approach and was just about to speak when Mr O'Grady shouted 'Mr Thompson it's time we had a talk'

Writing exercises on descriptive texts

Here are some descriptive writing tasks for you to practise writing.

1. Describe an old person who is well known to you.
2. Describe a birthday celebration for a member of your family.
3. Describe your thoughts and experiences on your first day at your present school or college.
4. Describe a place that you find frightening or unpleasant.
5. Describe a time when bad weather affected your neighbourhood.

4 ARGUMENTATIVE TEXTS

Reading argumentative texts

As their name suggests, argumentative texts are concerned with putting forward an argument in order to persuade the reader to share the point of view of the writer or to present a balanced view of a particular topic, giving the reader sufficient information to allow them to make up their own mind about the subject. Remember, an argument is not the same thing as a quarrel or a disagreement – the key point about good argumentative writing is that the writer has clear and firmly held points of view and their writing is logically structured and skilfully organised in order to convince the reader of their beliefs. Skilled writers will also attempt to counteract possible objections to the argument they are putting forward in order to make their argument more convincing.

Argumentative writing is often found in newspapers and magazines or on websites as well as in books and essays written by political organisations or pressure groups. When reading such writing, it is important that we pay close attention to the writer's arguments, not only the actual content but also the way in which the writing is put together and leads to its conclusion. This will not only help us follow what it is saying but also make it more likely that we will notice any illogicalities and unjustified statements which might suggest the writer is less knowledgeable than he or she wants to appear. It is also likely that the writer is biased in favour of a particular viewpoint and identifying this bias is an essential part of being able to make an impartial judgement on the writer's argument.

Practising how to write persuasively will of course help you to recognise all the features of an argumentative text when you encounter them in passages. But let's look at a few in more detail to help you disentangle an argument you are reading.

Topic sentences

In the same way as in informative writing, when writing out an argument, in each paragraph you should explore one idea relating to your main point and support it with whatever evidence you have available. Following this method of expounding your ideas often leads to a paragraph that contains one sentence in which the main idea is stated, and then the rest of the paragraph expands it, or repeats it with a different emphasis, or gives examples. The sentence in which the idea is stated is called the 'topic sentence' of the paragraph, and when reading an argument, picking the topic sentences out is often a helpful way of working through the writer's thoughts. It can be especially useful if you are trying to write a summary of the argument, when the requirement to write briefly means that you need to express the core of each idea without its related 'padding'.

Exercise 1

Look at the following passage and find the **two** reasons given in favour of having a rug and the **two** reasons against. Which sentence expresses each idea most briefly? Note that the topic sentence is not always the first – or the last – sentence of the paragraph.

> 'Shall we have a rug on the hall floor?' Dylan asked me. 'It would feel much warmer. At the moment the draught whistles in underneath the front door so that you can hardly feel the heat from the radiator. Even your precious rubber plant has brown edges to its leaves because of the draught.'
>
> 'But I hate vacuuming.' I made a face at him. 'You never do it, and the hall is a visitor's first impression of the house. I would be constantly worrying about whether the rug was clean. You always walk in straight from the garden without wiping your feet or taking your shoes off. It would get dirty too quickly.'
>
> 'The hall looks so dreary too. A rug would look pretty, especially if we bought one of those traditional Persian ones. I like those and we could choose one in colours to match the dining-room carpet.'
>
> 'The last time we went to your mother's you slipped on the Persian rug on the landing. You nearly tumbled headlong down the stairs, remember? Having a rug on a polished wooden floor is dangerous – they slide all the time and it's really difficult to fasten them down so that they stay in the right place. No, not a rug. If you don't like the wooden floor, we'll have to think about carpeting.'

Examples of argumentative texts

Here are two examples of argumentative writing. Each is attempting to encourage the reader to share the writer's point of view, and, especially in the case of the first, is written from a strongly held belief. As you read through them, think about exactly what it is that each writer wants you to believe.

Passage 1 was written (in 1999) by Linda McCartney who was a committed vegetarian (and the wife of Paul McCartney, one of the members of the Beatles). In the course of her argument she puts forward her own strongly held views and reinforces them with a secondary argument in which she encourages the readers, particularly those in the western world, to share her beliefs and explains that vegetarianism has become increasingly popular over recent years. Her tone is generally informal and colloquial; she writes in the first person and includes several references to her personal experience. However, she also supports these with statistics and other facts.

Passage 2 is a piece of sports journalism concerned with the argument that women tennis players should be given the same prize money as men. This is less of a personal argument than the first passage and although it soon becomes clear that the writer, Sue Mott, is opposed to the idea that male tennis stars deserve to be paid more than female players, she never explicitly states her own opinion. Instead of doing this, she uses the arguments of the players themselves, by quoting them directly, and, as a result, encourages readers to support their (and her) views. (N.B. Since 2007, when this article first appeared, the prize money at Wimbledon has been the same for men and women. The arguments over equal pay for men and women still continue, however, in other walks of life.)

Read through these passages closely and then answer the questions that follow each of them.

Passage 1

My New Frontier

The path of the vegetarian

By Linda McCartney

'If we are to address this problem of world hunger – and who else is responsible for it except those of us living here? – we need to effect a massive shift in where we feed the foods of our fields. Instead of feeding grain to livestock, we could feed the world by feeding the grain direct to people.'

It was the title of this magazine that caught my eye. A new frontier, it seemed so apt because that's what I'm facing now with my passion and drive to widen the appeal of vegetarianism.

If anything matters in my life besides my family it's this passion to spread this word – the V word – because so many lives depend upon it. And it's that that drives me, to try to save life.

So many people dismiss vegetarianism as if it's some form of mystic cult with no substance behind it, as if veggies are not quite right in the head. Believe me, I know. In the 20 years and more since Paul and I stopped eating animals, I've been called it all; cranky, loony, weirdo. There's not an insult in the book that hasn't been levelled at me because I eat differently from most people. Not that I'm complaining. If you strike out against convention with what is seen to be a new idea you have to expect the catcalls and suspicions, because people enjoy the comfort zone of a status quo, and change is always seen as challenging.

But the catcalls and jibes are lessening these days. Now, more and more people are starting to listen to us 'nutty' vegetarians, because science, medicine and economics have finally caught up with our philosophy and the disciples of tradition are realizing that the vegetarians make sense.

How so? Forget the emotional and moral arguments for a moment, and look at the hard facts. Medical studies all around the world are now proving that those who adopt a vegetarian diet are up to 40% less likely to die of cancer, and 30% less at risk to heart disease. The studies show that vegetarians are also less prone to high blood pressure, angina and diabetes.

I'm not making all this up. These are the findings of respected medical authorities. It's not me, but the Framingham Heart Study – the world's longest ongoing investigation into heart disease and diet, which has run since 1949 – that says, that on average, vegetarian men outlive other American men by six years. It's not me, but researchers at Boston's Brigham & Women's Hospital who claimed that women who eat meat every day are two and a half times more likely to have had colon cancer than women who ate meat sparingly or not at all.

➜

As I say, the word is now getting through, and throughout America more and more people are realizing that as death is not an option, medically a vegetarian diet makes sense. It is in part the growing realization of this that accounts for the fact that in the past ten years the number of vegetarians in the USA has almost doubled from 6.5 million in 1985 to 12.4 million now.

So there's one good reason for heeding this vegetarian argument – saving your life.

There are other, more altruistic reasons that are now gaining popularity with the one-time sceptics. Besides life-saving, vegetarianism is world-saving. As the people of this planet become more concerned about its potential longevity – and the fact that Greenpeace has had a 500% increase in its global membership, to five million members, over the past ten years suggests that they are concerned – the methods of meat production are coming increasingly under ecological scrutiny.

For instance, many young people are now finding it unacceptable that, in order to bring beef to the great American plate, a huge acreage of Central and South American rainforest has been razed and cleared to provide grazing land for cattle. At a time when tree cover of this earth is reducing rapidly, our kids need to know that for every 'quarterpounder' made from Central or South American beef, six square yards of rainforest is hewn for pasture.

Our kids also need to know that as they will inherit the planet they and their children are doomed to inherit a place where fresh water tables are dropping dramatically because 70% of all fresh American water is used in agriculture, and whereas it takes 25 gallons of that water to produce a pound of wheat, the University of California computed that it takes 5,214 gallons to produce a pound of beef.

Hopefully this new altruism will now extend to the way that we feed the world, because this is the new frontier that needs most to be crossed. According to UNICEF data, every 2.3 seconds a child dies on this planet because of hunger; since you began reading this sentence, and by the time you reach the end of it, four children will have died because they did not have enough to eat.

If there was ever a convincing argument for vegetarianism, it's right there because if we did not squander so much of our agricultural resources on meat production, these children would not die.

We waste so much to gain so little as so many others die with nothing. We waste 16 pounds of grain in livestock feed to produce one single pound of beef. We feed 80% of the corn grown in the USA not to people, but to livestock.

If we are to address this problem of world hunger – and who else is responsible for it except those of us living here? – we need to effect a massive shift in where we feed the foods of our fields. Instead of feeding grain to livestock, we could feed the world by feeding the grain direct to people.

And I'm not asking anyone to suffer here. If, for instance, Americans reduced their intake of meat by just 10% – if just one in every ten meals was meatless – that would free up enough land, water and energy from growing livestock feed to adequately feed 40 million starving people. And that's official, from the Worldwatch Institute.

The point is that this problem is not going to go away; the problem is going to get worse as the population explodes in the next century like never before. More people are going to have less to eat, and we have to find new ways of feeding them.

It appears to me that as you can grow 40,000 lbs of potatoes or 10,000 lbs of beans on an acre of prime land that would produce just 250 lbs of beef, one of these new ways has to be a major shift away from meat-eating.

Of course, to argue for this change is to invite the catcalls again because by asking people to change their eating habits we are asking them to change tradition and people like to cling to tradition.

Tradition, the way it is, is only an idea that has had widespread acceptance for a protracted period of time. But now we have to find new, better ideas. Just because something is a tradition does not, in itself, make it a good idea. It used to be a tradition for women not to have the vote. It used to be a tradition in my husband's home town of Liverpool to ship black people from Africa to America as slaves. These were not good ideas and new, better ideas overcame them.

And I have faith that these new ideas for the way we eat will change the way it is to the way it should be. I have faith because so many people who might once have mocked vegetarianism, are now opening up to these new ideas. The very presence of this magazine in the market proves that minds are opening to the new possibilities.

And that change is coming fast. In England, as I write, newspapers have just reported the findings of a poll of teenage schoolgirls that has found that 57% of those age 14 and under are now claiming to be vegetarian. Of these kids, 82% said they have stopped eating meat because they don't believe that animals should be killed for food.

Such poll findings were unheard of ten years ago. But then, ten years ago, who would have said that the Berlin Wall would come down, that the Soviet bloc would collapse under pressure for democracy, or that Nelson Mandela would go from a prison to a presidency?

But ten years ago, I'd have laughed if anyone told me I could write a vegetarian cookbook that one person would buy, let alone 360,000 people who bought it worldwide. Ten years ago I'd have scoffed at the very idea that frozen vegetarian food with my face on it would be selling in the supermarkets of California, or that 60 million meals of the same food would have sold in the UK last year. Or that we could create meals from wheat that taste so like meat you wouldn't know the difference.

Ten years ago I wouldn't have believed you if you'd asked me to create ready-made vegetarian meals for Japan, Sweden, Germany, Holland and Australia. There's no demand, I'd have said, people aren't that interested. Japan? But they're interested, and are asking me now.

Ten years ago I wouldn't have said 'there's a food revolution going on'.

Ten years from now I hope we'll say 'We told you so.'

Exercise 2

1 Read Passage 1 'The path of the vegetarian' carefully and then explain:

- what the writer thinks are the benefits of people becoming vegetarian
- why vegetarianism has become more popular over the past ten years.

Start by writing down as briefly as possible the separate benefits and reasons, leaving out all the repetitions and 'padding'. Then put them into your own words as far as possible, linking them to reproduce the writer's sequence of thought. You now have a summary of the main ideas of the passage.

2 By referring to the whole article, explain, as fully as you can, how Linda McCartney sets out to persuade her readers that her views are right. You should write about:
- the content of her article, in particular the examples she gives, the order she gives them in and the way she moves from one to the next
- her tone of voice and the language she uses.

Extension task

Build up your summary of the article 'The path of the vegetarian' with as much as you like of the writer's extra material, adding some ideas of your own if you wish, to make an argumentative essay of your own.

Passage 2

Serve and volley – women are worth the same lolly

By Sue Mott

The Americans have always done it. The Australians started it recently. The French are just pretending to do it. The British won't do it at all. All socio-cultural history is here, wrapped up neatly in the hot-potato issue of whether women tennis players should be paid equally to men.

This very morning Wimbledon will unveil its prize money structure for the Championships this summer. Will they crack? Will they succumb to the charming offensive being waged by Billie Jean King, former Wimbledon champion and feminist campaigner, and a host of women players who complain with some bitterness that this is an issue of social injustice?

'I really hope I am the last woman player in history ever to be paid unequally,' said Venus Williams, the 2005 champion.

'Women's tennis players are getting as many sponsors and media coverage as men, and our TV ratings at the Grand Slams are pretty much equal to and often better than the men, so I don't understand the rationale for paying the men more than us,' said Maria Sharapova, the 2004 champion.

'The fact that two of the grandest stages for women's sport, Wimbledon and Roland Garros, still do not treat women equal to the men is a black mark on the sport,' said Chris Evert, three times Wimbledon champion.

Oh girls, you do know what you are letting yourself in for, don't you? It was only a few years ago that the men in charge of the cricketing establishment at Lord's were forced to admit women as members to the MCC. These old reactionaries and their like will now be out in force, barracking for the supremacy of man, and, specifically man in a necktie, with the unalterable belief that women are fluffy, frivolous and fundamentally unequal. Wimbledon is one of their last resorts.

They have survived all this time on the quality control argument. Men play more sets. Men have greater strength in depth. This is absolutely, unarguably, true. Men do play more sets, best of five, instead of best of three. They are not always gorgeous sets, they may be execrable sets, but they are there in number. As for the depth of the women's game, it is pretty low. Not enough to let British players qualify straight into the main draw, but low nevertheless. Billie Jean's answer: 'So what?' And I'm with her.

So what? In the final analysis, Wimbledon is Wimbledon, it sells out every year, vastly oversubscribed, not because the men have strength in depth, not because women play three, five or 27 sets and not even because of the strawberry cream teas on sale there. It sells because it is Wimbledon, a unique, traditional, highly-tuned, economically-sustainable event, featuring (crucially) men and women. No one begs for men's Wimbledon tickets. They beg for Wimbledon tickets, men or women, irrespective.

'As an argument, women's labour productivity just doesn't do it,' said Larry Scott, the WTA chief executive. 'We're not manufacturing ball bearings here. We're in the entertainment business.' He is right. Women are fundamental to the Wimbledon experience, history, profit. It is a mean-minded effort to deny them parity.

The US sees that. Sports equality is enshrined in their law. Australians (of all people) have come to see that; equal pay at Flinders Park was granted in 2001. Only old Europe is lagging behind. Roland Garros, the stadium where the French Open Championships are held, is paying their men's and women's champions equal money this year, both earning €940,000 (£650,550), but sneakily the French are then underpaying all the previous round female winners in comparison with the men.

At least the British have been brazen about it. Last year, Roger Federer won £630,000 while Venus Williams took home five per cent less, £600,000. It is clearly not a money thing. Wimbledon could afford £30,000 in the context of their £25 million profit. It is a message thing. The girls aren't quite good enough. Know your place sweetie, second best.

'Sport is just a microcosm of life. It's a cultural thing,' reckons Billie Jean. 'It's about the top group, the power group, not wanting to let go. But it's not right. It's not justice. They should do the right thing. I am really, really hoping that the All England Club chairman, Tim Phillips, who I adore by the way, decides to leave equal pay for women as his legacy. Even if his cronies give him a bad time, I hope he makes a symbolic statement.' Phillips was made aware of her feelings, that he could single-handedly send a socio-economic message throughout the globe. 'You reckon?' he said enigmatically.

All right, it might be overstating the case. To pay more money to a bunch of multi-millionairesses, with cars to match their handbags, seems unnecessary. But at the risk of sounding like a union shop steward, it is not the money – it's the principle. Equality is a perception thing.

Sport could, should, take a hand in suggesting women deserve equal treatment. The knock-on effect could be bountiful.

Giving Venus Williams another £30,000 to buy more belts is not going to change the world, but saying 'We believe women deserve to be treated as well as men' does send a symbolic message to those places on earth where women are seen politically as very much second class citizens.

'Do the right thing,' said Billie Jean to the UK, a country that still thinks women should clear off golf courses on a Sunday. She may have to be a 21st-century suffragette a little longer.

Exercise 3

1 Read Passage 2 'Serve and volley' carefully and then explain:
- the arguments for and against women and men tennis players being paid equal prize money
- what the writer says about Wimbledon and the tennis championships held there.

Follow the same stages as in Exercise 2, Question 1 and the Extension task. In selecting the points to list, you do not need to distinguish between the people who are quoted, as the writer is using their views as part of her own argument.

2 From your reading of Passage 2, comment on how the writer puts across her views on:
- the issue of equal prize money for men and women tennis players
- the attitudes of the English sporting establishment and those who represent it.

In your answer you should look closely at the content of her article, the tone of her writing and the words and phrases that she uses.

The difference between opinions and facts

Look back at Passage 1 'The path of the vegetarian' by Linda McCartney on page 47. As we have already seen, this is a deeply felt piece urging people to share the writer's beliefs, but it is stuffed full of facts, definite figures, statistics, names of people and places. All these contribute to the impression that what the writer is saying must be right, as it can all be proved.

When you are writing, you should have researched your topic and know quite a lot about it; but when you are reading a piece you are unlikely to be an expert on the subject. Often you rely on the writer to tell you the relevant facts, and you have to take them on trust while you are following the argument. Or do you? How can you tell when something is not a provable fact but only an opinion of the writer, inserted to move the argument on?

The same piece by McCartney is also stuffed full of her opinions. Can you see them? Some of them are clearly signalled, for example:

> It appears to me that as you can grow 40,000 lbs of potatoes or 10,000 lbs of beans on an acre of prime land that would produce just 250 lbs of beef, one of these new ways has to be a major shift away from meat-eating.

The facts about the amount of potatoes or beans try to camouflage it, and the use of 'has to be' makes it sound definite, but it is still an opinion of the writer that 'one of these new ways has to be a major shift …' and it is signalled by 'It appears to me'.

But what about:

> If there was ever a convincing argument for vegetarianism, it's right there because if we did not squander so much of our agricultural resources on meat production, these children would not die.

Fact or opinion? The emotive word 'squander' should make you pause, and the conditional ('if') clause, and it is rather too like a sweeping emotional reference as mentioned on page 62 to be completely convincing. But it is presented as a statement of fact.

Remember that identifying the difference between a fact and an opinion is not the same as agreeing with what is said or not. You can agree wholeheartedly with the idea of vegetarianism and still recognise that the belief that less meat production would save children, however widely held, is a belief, not a fact.

Change of direction/focus

Recognising the organisation of an argumentative piece is essential to understanding the movement through the argument. The commonest signposts that you may use are: *Firstly*, *Moreover*, *Finally* (this is discussed in more detail on page 62), but many writers try to use more subtle markers. For instance, in 'The path of the vegetarian', how did Linda McCartney signal her move from talking about the benefits of vegetarianism to her belief that vegetarianism is becoming more popular?

As you read, look out for the different ways of linking points and marking a shift of direction or focus. For example, another example of the way in which a writer subtly shifts the focus of her argument is found in 'Serve and volley' where Sue Mott picks up on the quotation from Billie Jean King, 'So what?' and uses the same phrase herself to introduce the following paragraph in order to develop her argument.

Further reading exercises on argumentative/persuasive writing

Read Passage 3. To help you understand the writer's point of view as a whole, one sentence that sums it up has been highlighted. As you read the passage for the first time, try to think how each of the paragraphs takes a different aspect of that idea and develops it. Then read it again and answer the questions that follow.

Passage 3

From *Why I Write*

1 The Spanish war and other events in 1936–37 turned the scale and thereafter I knew where I stood. Every line of serious work that I have written since 1936 has been written, directly or indirectly, against totalitarianism and for democratic socialism, as I understand it. It seems to me nonsense, in a period like our own, to think that one can avoid writing of such subjects. Everyone writes of them in one guise or another. It is simply a question of which side one takes and what approach one follows. And the more one is conscious of one's political bias, the more chance one has of acting politically without sacrificing one's aesthetic and intellectual integrity.

2 **What I have most wanted to do throughout the past ten years is to make political writing into an art.** My starting point is always a feeling of partisanship, a sense of injustice. When I sit down to write a book, I do not say to myself, 'I am going to produce a work of art'. I write it because there is some lie that I want to expose, some fact to which I want to draw attention, and my initial concern is to get a hearing. But I could not do the work of writing a book, or even a long magazine article, if it were not also an aesthetic experience. Anyone who cares to examine my work will see that even when it is downright propaganda it contains much that a full-time politician would consider irrelevant. I am not able, and do not want, completely to abandon the world view that I acquired in childhood. So long as I remain alive and well I shall continue to feel strongly about prose style, to love the surface of the earth, and to take a pleasure in solid objects and scraps of useless information. It is no use trying to suppress that side of myself. The job is to reconcile my ingrained likes and dislikes with the essentially public, non-individual activities that this age forces on all of us.

3 It is not easy. It raises problems of construction and of language, and it raises in a new way the problem of truthfulness. Let me give just one example of the cruder kind of difficulty that arises. My book about the Spanish civil war, *Homage to Catalonia*, is of course a frankly political book, but in the main it is written with a certain detachment and regard for form. I did try very hard in it to tell the whole truth without violating my literary instincts. But among other things it contains a long chapter, full of newspaper quotations and the like, defending the Trotskyists who were accused of plotting with Franco. Clearly such a chapter, which after a year or two would lose its interest for any ordinary reader, must ruin the book. A critic whom I respect read me a lecture about it. 'Why did you put in all that stuff?' he said. 'You've turned what might have been a good book into journalism.' What he said was true, but I could not have done otherwise. I happened to know, what very few people in England had been allowed to know, that innocent

men were being falsely accused. If I had not been angry about that I should never have written the book.

4 In one form or another this problem comes up again. The problem of language is subtler and would take too long to discuss. I will only say that of late years I have tried to write less picturesquely and more exactly. In any case I find that by the time you have perfected any style of writing, you have always outgrown it. *Animal Farm* was the first book in which I tried, with full consciousness of what I was doing, to fuse political purpose and artistic purpose into one whole. I have not written a novel for seven years, but I hope to write another fairly soon. It is bound to be a failure, every book is a failure, but I do know with some clarity what kind of book I want to write.

5 Looking back through the last page or two, I see that I have made it appear as though my motives in writing were wholly public-spirited. I don't want to leave that as the final impression. All writers are vain, selfish, and lazy, and at the very bottom of their motives there lies a mystery. Writing a book is a horrible, exhausting struggle, like a long bout of some painful illness. One would never undertake such a thing if one were not driven on by some demon whom one can neither resist nor understand. For all one knows that demon is simply the same instinct that makes a baby squall for attention. And yet it is also true that one can write nothing readable unless one constantly struggles to efface one's own personality. Good prose is like a windowpane. I cannot say with certainty which of my motives are the strongest, but I know which of them deserve to be followed. And looking back through my work, I see that it is invariably where I lacked a *political* purpose that I wrote lifeless books and was betrayed into purple passages, sentences without meaning, decorative adjectives and humbug generally.

George Orwell

Exercise 4

1 What historical event led to the writer realising the principles on which he should write? Is there an event in more recent times that you feel could have had the same effect? Why? (paragraph 1)
2 According to the writer, what advantage has he gained from being aware of his political bias? (paragraph 1)
3 What first motivates the writer to start writing a book? (paragraph 2)
4 What else does the writer consider to be important to him? Why does that make him say that his work contains much that a politician would consider 'irrelevant'? (paragraph 2)
5 What were 'the essentially public, non-individual activities that this age forces on all of us'? Are there any equivalents today? Why does the

writer feel he has to 'reconcile my ingrained likes and dislikes' with them? (paragraph 2)

6 Why did the writer include the long chapter full of newspaper quotations in *Homage to Catalonia*? (paragraph 3)
7 What did the critic mean when he said that the writer had 'turned what might have been a good book into journalism'? What does the comment tell us about the critic? (paragraph 3)
8 In what ways does the writer say his style has changed over the years? (paragraph 4)
9 In the final paragraph, the writer introduces another motivation for writing, which he thinks is common to all writers. Explain what it is and why he calls it a 'demon'.
10 Explain what the writer means when he says: 'Good prose is like a windowpane.'
11 Which of the writer's motivations for writing do you think he himself considers the most important? Why?

Summary task

a Make notes of what Passage 3 tells us about why George Orwell writes and about the beliefs he holds.
b Now write a summary of what Passage 3 tells us about why George Orwell writes and about the beliefs he holds. You should write about 250–300 words, and use your own words as far as possible.

Writing summaries

Being able to summarise information from something you have read is a key skill in English and is one that can be used in all walks of life. To produce a good summary you need to use first your reading skills, and then your writing skills. Here is some advice on how to approach producing a summary, especially if you are doing so as an examination exercise.

- The aim in producing a summary is to identify and pull together the key points that are relevant to the purpose for which you are writing. Including irrelevant information would mean that anyone reading your summary would be confused. Therefore, in order for the reader to be able to understand the relevant information clearly, it is important that you have carefully selected the appropriate details.
- So the first stage in writing a summary is to read the original article through so that you know what it is about.
- Next you need to fix clearly in your mind the precise requirements of the summary. In real life you would know why you are writing, for example to tell a friend the plot of a film, but in an examination this means looking carefully at the question and making sure you understand what is being asked for. Often a question asks for two related but separate aspects, such as the problems caused by flooding, and the steps taken to prevent them.
- Now read through the passage again and make a list of the key points you wish to include. You may find it helpful to go through the passage

first, underlining or highlighting any words or phrases that have a direct relevance to the topic of your summary. Use as a heading the overall topic of the summary you are writing – or make two columns for the two separate aspects.
- The examination paper asks you to present this list to be assessed separately. You should be careful to write down the complete point each time. Each separate fact that you list has to make complete sense on its own. If your summary is for another purpose, this list can be in note form and only as full as you need in order to work with the points. Don't be tempted to omit this stage as it is fundamental to writing a good summary.
- Watch out for repetitions of the same point in different words. If the passage says 'You must list each point in full' and then 'Be careful not to leave out part of a point', it is saying the same thing, first positively and then negatively. You should not include both ways of making the one point.
- Watch out also for extensions to the point in the form of examples or for emphasis. There is only one point in the whole of: 'Make as much noise as you possibly can, by shouting, screaming, banging on the wall, jumping heavily up and down, anything you can think of to attract attention.' (But be careful to get it in full: 'Make a loud noise to attract attention', not just 'Make a loud noise'.)
- Watch out also for unnecessary descriptive padding that can be omitted without affecting the main sense of the point, such as lists of adjectives, or similes or metaphors intended to make the original point clearer.

Up till now you have been using your reading skills to select a list of relevant points – and at least half of the credit you will gain for a good summary is for the selection and relevance of your material. Only at this stage should you turn to using your writing skills to produce the actual summary.

- Once you have your list(s) of points, it may be necessary to reorganise and manipulate the details to ensure that they are in a logical order. Remember that the points may well occur in the original passage in a different order as the focus of your summary is likely to be slightly different from that of the original writer. It is important that you have a clear overview in your mind of what you intend to write before you start to organise the notes you have made.
- As you plan how best to arrange the points you have identified, you are likely to notice that some of them, although separate, contain very similar ideas. Try to combine such points, as this will give a clearer focus to what you are writing, and practically it also helps you to keep within any word limit. Combining points in this way is called *synthesis* and is a high-level summary skill.
- Finally, you are ready to think about writing out your own version of the summarised points. Examination summary questions will usually require you to keep to a particular word limit and it is important that you observe this word limit as closely as possible. However, it is equally important that you include a sensible spread of points, so don't use 75 per cent of your available words on the first three points in your list when you have a total of ten points to include altogether! One way to avoid this is to try

to use roughly the same number of words for each point; for example, if your word limit is 250 words and you have 10 points to make, then you should allow about 25 words for each point. Not every point will need 25 words, so you will have a few extra for a point that needs stating a little more lengthily.

- Avoid lengthy and irrelevant introductory comments – or any introduction or conclusion at all if possible; your readers are only interested in assimilating the key relevant points as swiftly as possible. Do not make any comments about the material; your job when writing a summary is to convey the writer's ideas as clearly as possible. Do not add any material of your own; doing so will distract the reader from the main points.
- Write the summary using your own words as far as possible. It is not a good idea to lift whole phrases and sentences from the original or to fill your version with quotations from it. If you rely too much on the words of the writer, you are not making your understanding of the passage clear to a reader; this is particularly important when you are writing a summary as part of an examination.
- However, using your own words does not mean that you need to find a synonym for every word of the original; for example, you do not have to reword technical vocabulary. 'Own words' is often as much a matter of re-structuring the sentences and linking them coherently as it is of vocabulary. Even doing something as straightforward as turning a passive construction from the original into an active one in your own version is enough to show that you have understood the material.
- Remember that your version should show a clear overview of the topic and be clearly focused. If all the points you have identified relate to the same topic, then they should all form part of one paragraph. If you are writing a summary containing two topics, then you may find a paragraph for each is the most sensible structure. But remember that you will have to include some kind of link or bridge between those two paragraphs so that your version is a single piece – you cannot insert a second heading halfway through!

The other half of the credit for a summary comes from the way you have presented the points and linked them together to form a coherent statement of the original writer's text. Grammatical or spelling errors affect the clarity of your statement and are a demerit.

The above method might seem a little time-consuming, especially if you are writing a summary under timed conditions as an examination answer. However, going through this process is likely to ensure that you show a full understanding of the relevant points in the original passage. You will probably have at least 30 minutes to answer this question in an examination; you will be required to write only a limited number of words – it does not take very long to write out 180 words, for example, *once you know what it is you are going to write!* Careful preparation will put you in this position; two-thirds of the time you have available, at least, should be spent in reading and preparation; writing the summary is straightforward after that.

Bias and emotive language

To show *bias* means to show a preference towards a particular subject or thing and, in particular, to try to influence someone to share your personal opinion in a non-objective way.

It is, therefore, important that, when you are reading a piece of argumentative or persuasive writing, you take into account any possible bias that is shown by the writer.

In some cases, it is quite easy to identify the writer's bias. For example, if you are reading a newspaper that is known to support a particular political party, then it is likely that any comments made by its journalists on matters of national or international policy are likely to be written to endorse the views of the political party that the owners of the newspaper support. Similarly, it is likely that a local community newspaper, when reporting on a sporting event involving a team from its own community will present details of the game in order to present as positive a picture as possible of the performance of the local team.

Another example is if you are reading an article about the health effects of smoking and you notice in the small print at the bottom that the article was sponsored by a leading cigarette manufacturer, then it is likely that the writer's conclusions will be influenced by his or her need not to damage the profits of the company that commissioned the article! These are all examples of bias shown in the selection of the content, by including or omitting certain facts or opinions.

However, not all examples are so easy to spot. In order to persuade you to share their points of view, skilful writers will use all the resources of language that they have at their command to influence you. In particular, they will try to influence readers in a subconscious way by choosing words that have particular associations or connotations in order to produce an emotional rather than a strictly logical response. Such a technique is known as using *emotive* language.

In Chapter 3, we looked at synonyms and saw how careful choice of vocabulary allowed a writer to create a precise description. In argumentative essays, the range of synonyms available to a writer of English allows a writer (or speaker) to influence a reader's (or listener's) response to a particular point of view. For example, look at the following sentences:

- On his return from college, Francis received a cordial welcome from members of his family.
- On his return from college, Francis received a hearty welcome from members of his family.

The only difference between these two sentences is in the adjective describing the welcome that Francis was given and nearly all readers would agree that a *hearty* welcome is something much warmer than a *cordial* one which has the associations of being something quite formal and polite. However, the word *cordial* derives from the Latin word *cor* which means *heart* and so, in theory, the two words *cordial* and *hearty* should mean the same thing. The fact is that, over a period of time, the two words have taken on different connotations and, like many words that have come into English from Latin, *cordial* has acquired more formal associations.

Here is another example:

- The teacher wrote in Lee's report that he was a very self-confident and respectful student.
- The teacher wrote in Lee's report that he was a very arrogant and aloof student.

Again, only two words have been changed between the first and second sentence. However, the meaning has changed significantly. The words *self-confident* and *respectful* in the first sentence are both neutral words and contribute to the sense that in the teacher's opinion, Lee is a good member of the class. However, by substituting the words *arrogant* and *aloof* in the second sentence, the teacher has created the impression that Lee's attitude is negative and potentially disruptive and that he may well be a bad influence in the classroom.

Exercise 5

Here is a description of an unpleasant character from Anthony Trollope's novel *Barchester Towers*. Read through the description carefully and then:

a explain the associations of each of the words or phrases underlined and how they contribute to your attitude towards Mr Slope

b replace each of these words or phrases with other words in order to present Mr Slope as a likeable and pleasant character.

> Mr Slope is tall, and not ill made. His feet and hands are large, as has ever been the case with all his family, but he has a broad chest and wide shoulders to carry off these excrescences, and on the whole his figure is good. His countenance, however, is not specially prepossessing. His hair is lank, and of a dull pale reddish hue. It is always formed into three straight lumpy masses, each brushed with admirable precision, and cemented with much grease; two of them adhere closely to the sides of his face, and the other lies at right angles above them. He wears no whiskers, and is always punctiliously shaven. His face is nearly of the same colour as his hair, though perhaps a little redder: it is not unlike beef, – beef, however, one would say, of a bad quality. His forehead is capacious and high, but square and heavy, and unpleasantly shining. His mouth is large, though his lips are thin and bloodless; and his big, prominent, pale brown eyes inspire anything but confidence. His nose, however, is his redeeming feature: it is pronounced straight and well-formed; though I myself should have liked it better if it did not possess a somewhat spongy, porous appearance, as though it had been cleverly formed out of a red coloured cork.
>
> I never could endure to shake hands with Mr Slope. A cold, clammy perspiration always exudes from him, the small drops are ever to be seen standing on his brow, and his friendly grasp is unpleasant.

Writing to argue and persuade

The examples we have looked at in this chapter have been concerned with presenting the reader with a clearly held point of view and are intended to lead to the reader being convinced by the writer's argument. However, the different writers have approached this task in varying ways. For example, Linda McCartney writes in the first person and presents a personal argument, supported either by references to events in her own life or by referring to statistics and comments from other sources. Sue Mott's newspaper article, however, presents its arguments mainly through making references to the views and theories of other people who are closely concerned with the topics about which she is writing in order to persuade the readers to share her view that women players should be given equal prize money to that of men.

Although most argumentative writing has the intention of convincing the reader of the truth of the writer's point of view, it is not always concerned with a controversial topic – remember the point that was made at the beginning of this chapter: an argument is not the same thing as a quarrel. When producing your own pieces of argumentative writing, it is important that you have the purpose of your writing clearly in mind and that you use a tone and vocabulary suited to that purpose. For example, if you are presenting an argument setting out a personal principle or belief, you can most effectively convey this to your readers by adopting a balanced, serious tone and using precise, rational vocabulary in which you set out the facts clearly and logically. However, if you are attempting to persuade your readers to share your view on a controversial topic, then it is likely that you will choose to use more emotively toned vocabulary and to set out consciously to discredit the arguments of those who might hold opposing ideas.

In either case it is of the utmost importance that you carefully research your topic and plan the order of what you intend to say, before you actually start to write.

Tips for argumentative/persuasive writing

Let's look at the points above more closely.

Organisation

- Before starting to write, it is important that you organise your points logically and in the best possible order to make your argument convincing. You should start with an *introduction* in which you state clearly the main proposition of your argument. The essay should then develop logically, paragraph by paragraph. In each paragraph you should explore one idea relating to your main point and support it with whatever evidence you have available. Each paragraph should, therefore, lead into the next until you have fully completed your argument; it is then important that you finish with a *conclusion* in which you sum up the key points of your argument in order to reinforce the proposition with which you began. Remember: writing an argumentative essay becomes much easier if you know what your conclusion is going to be before you start to write!

- As you write – particularly if you are presenting a controversial argument – it is important to be thinking of counter arguments that might be made by people with an opposing point of view. You will strengthen your own case if you give consideration to these counter arguments and then produce convincing arguments against them. Such considerations can either be included paragraph by paragraph, or you could spend the first part of your essay discounting your opponents' arguments before presenting your own case in the second half, leading into your conclusion.
- In order to make your argument convincing it is important that you have researched your topic carefully and have good knowledge of it so that you can support your arguments with references to facts, statistics and other authorities. However, it is important that these supports are convincing and credible. You should avoid substituting sweeping emotional references (such as 'doing this would lead to everyone feeling much happier') as they cannot be logically proven and are likely to diminish the force of your argument. Similarly, you should try to avoid oversimplifying your arguments and making unsubstantiated generalisations ('surely, anyone can see that this is a most sensible idea').
- It is important that your essay follows a logical development. In order to make this more effective, there are various techniques for linking sentences and paragraphs that provide the reader with signposts towards your intended conclusion. Here are some of the more commonly used techniques:
  - In order to indicate that you are producing a logically structured argument, flag this up at the start of your essay. Once you have made your introductory statement, begin the next paragraph with 'Firstly' or 'First of all'; for example 'First of all, I shall consider …'. You can then link the next paragraph by starting with the word, 'Secondly' or, if you want to sound less mechanical, 'The next point to be considered…'.
  - Other words which signpost the development of your argument and which can be used effectively as paragraph openers are, 'Furthermore', 'Moreover', 'In addition'.
  - A change in the direction of your argument – for example, when you are about to introduce and consider possible opposing views – can be signposted by opening a paragraph with words such as 'However', 'Nevertheless', 'On the other hand' and even, 'But'.
  - Prepare readers for the conclusion of your essay by starting the relevant paragraph(s) with, 'Finally', 'In conclusion', 'To conclude', 'In summary', 'To summarise all the preceding arguments', or, if the argument has been argued in a tightly logical manner, 'Thus'.

Technical skills

There are various techniques that you can use to make your argumentative writing more effective. Here are a few of them:

Rhetorical questions

Rhetorical questions are questions directed at an audience that do not require a direct answer but which are intended to influence the audience into agreeing with the point being made through the question. For example:

> But is punishing every student in the school really the best way to deal with this small outbreak of vandalism? (This is expecting the answer *no*.)
>
> Wouldn't everyone present welcome an extra day's holiday this week? (This is expecting the answer *yes*.)

Repetition

This is the technique whereby words or phrases are repeated throughout the essay to emphasise certain points or ideas. For example:

> There is only one way to put an end to this; only one way to dispose of this particular threat and only one chance to do so before it is too late.

There is a good example of the repetition of a phrase for emphasis at the end of 'The path of the vegetarian' – did you notice it?

This technique is often particularly effective if the repetition is of words from the beginning used again in the conclusion to remind readers of the opening proposition and round off the argument.

Hyperbole

This is deliberate exaggeration to emphasise a particular point; it can be very effective but should not be overdone. Here is an example:

> Despite asking thousands of times for the work to be completed, by the end of the day, the teacher was still waiting for everyone to finish.

Litotes

Litotes is the opposite of hyperbole and is when a writer or speaker uses a form of understatement to emphasise a point. For example:

> It is not an easy task to discover a cure for cancer. (The writer means, of course, that it is a very difficult task.)

Parallelism

This is the use of parallel sentence structures in which successive clauses or sentences follow a similar pattern, allowing the reader to concentrate on what is being said. For example:

> The principles we live by reflect the values of those with whom we work, those who are in positions of authority over us and the larger society of which we are all a part.

Punctuation: semi-colons and colons

These two punctuation devices should not be confused. Each has specific purposes and the ability to use them correctly and with confidence is one of the marks of a skilled writer.

Semi-colons are used for two main purposes:

- To separate two main clauses when they could otherwise be joined by a conjunction such as *and* or *but*. For example: *Banning traffic from the town centre will make life safer for pedestrians; it will also make the area much quieter.* (These two statements could also be joined by using *and*, however the use of the semi-colon emphasises the second half of the sentence and gives it equal force with the first.)
- To separate clauses or phrases in a list. (Remember: single words in lists are separated by commas.) For example: *The government must make up its mind what should be done: it can ban all traffic in the town centre at all times; it can ban cars and lorries using the town centre on weekdays only; it can allow commercial vehicles but ban private ones completely or it can leave things exactly as they are.*

Colons are used for three main purposes. These are:

- To separate two statements where the second expands on the meaning of the first. For example: *His heart sank as he approached the town centre: the traffic was at a complete standstill and there was no indication that it would be moving again for at least an hour.*
- To introduce a number of items or options in a list. For example: *The government must make up its mind what should be done: it can ban all traffic in the town centre at all times; it can ban cars and lorries using the town centre on weekdays only; it can allow commercial vehicles but ban private ones completely or it can leave things exactly as they are.*
- To introduce a speech or a quotation. For example: *Hamlet: To be or not to be, that is the question.*

Punctuation exercise

Rewrite the following passage inserting semi-colons and colons as necessary.

> The sun was shining it was a fine day. Samuel awoke drew back the curtains in his bedroom looked happily at the glittering sea in the distance and decided that he would call his friends and suggest they spent the day at the beach. He thought about what he would have to take with him and started to pack his bag it was not particularly large so he knew that he had to think carefully. Finally he decided on the following a bottle of ice cold water his bathing costume and a towel some sandwiches for his lunch a large bottle of sun lotion his baseball cap to protect his head from the sun and a pair of sunglasses.

Argumentative writing exercises

1 There has been a proposal to demolish an old factory on the outskirts of your town and to build a large leisure centre in its place. An editorial in your local newspaper has opposed this plan and argued that the site would be better used for a new hospital. The Editor has asked readers to write in with their comments.

   Write a letter to the Editor in which you argue the case for one or other of the buildings. You should consider the merits of both before making your final recommendation.

2 'There's men's work and there's women's work.' How far do you agree with this statement? Argue your point of view.

3 A friend who belongs to an older generation has no time for modern technology such as cell phones or computers. Write a letter in which you try to persuade him or her of the advantages of owning one of these objects.

4 'Young people have too much freedom these days.' Do you agree or disagree with this statement? Argue your point of view.

Extension task

This next task involves both reading and writing skills. This section contains a collection of articles both for and against the controversial practice of animal testing, which provide a resource for writing an extended essay either opposing or supporting the use of animals for scientific and medical research. You may find it useful to work through the steps given in Exercise 2 on pages 49–50 before starting your essay. You may, if you wish, extend your research and include any other information that you find to support your argument.

(It is suggested that before setting the above, or similar tasks, teachers select from and edit the material to suit the aptitude and ability of the students in their class. The information contained here could also be used for a class oral activity such as a formal debate.)

Animal experiments

Animal testing a necessary research tool, for now

Sept. 3, 2006 12:00 AM

As a veterinarian and someone who has spent three decades in biomedical research in academia and the pharmaceutical industry, I know that animal research saves lives and I am concerned by deceptive claims from extremist groups about the need for animal research.

Animal studies continue to be necessary for advancing human and animal health and have played a vital role in virtually every major medical advance. This includes lifesaving drugs and vaccines, new surgical procedures and improved diagnosis of disease.

A hallmark of humanity is our ability to care about other species. It is understandably difficult for people to reconcile this empathy with support of animal studies for medical advances that cure disease and improve the quality of life.

Animal extremists prey on this discomfort and count on society's general lack of scientific insight to advance their agenda. These extremists knowingly misrepresent the ability of computers and emerging scientific techniques to serve as viable substitutes for animal studies.

Government regulations around the world require that new drugs, vaccines and surgical implants first be tested in animals for potential toxic reactions. Beyond these formal legal requirements, research into the root causes of disease at the genetic level and how diseases become resistant to current treatments cannot be simulated by computer programs or duplicated in test tubes.

Although present-day technology cannot yet replace many types of animal research, the research community is committed to finding new ways to reduce and replace animal testing. This ethical commitment is embodied in strict animal welfare protocols at most university, government and industrial laboratories.

In addition to humane considerations, the economic and logistical advantages of replacing animal testing are compelling. Animal studies are time-consuming and resource-intensive. If meaningful alternatives existed, companies could save hundreds of millions of dollars in facilities and personnel costs.

Opposition to all animal testing would require a life without drugs, vaccines, painkillers, anaesthetics and surgery. It would demand a rejection of all federally mandated Food and Drug Administration and Environmental Protection Agency tests that ensure the safe consumption of products in our homes and workplaces, ranging from the testing of components used in computers and cell phones to plastic wraps and chemical additives in our foods and drinks. In short, it would require a lifestyle far removed from that enjoyed by most people, particularly the jet-setting celebrities who oppose animal research.

Reducing complex issues to oversimplified sound bites encourages the thinking that wearing a lapel ribbon is a substitute for education and dedication to seeking solutions. Research scientists, physicians and veterinarians face tough moral and ethical issues in this pursuit and take these responsibilities seriously.

Concern about animal welfare can take very different forms. Some people are offended by the use of leather and fur as fashion accessories but accept that medical research must unavoidably use animals until viable alternatives are found. Some groups argue persuasively against intensive farming practices but, again, recognize the need for animals in medical research. I recently signed a petition in Arizona calling for reform in the raising of veal calves.

My advice is that people carefully consider not just whether or not a group share their beliefs, but whether or not they behave in an ethical manner. The tactics used by opponents of animal testing have included false claims about the alternatives and misinformation aimed at provoking community concerns about potential disasters.

Well-funded national groups often disguise their involvement to make it appear as if local citizens are leading the effort. In May, the Arizona Republic uncovered deceptive methods and use of false names by a leading opponent of a local drug-development facility in an attempt to camouflage ties to People for the Ethical Treatment of Animals and involvement in other protest campaigns.

Of greatest concern are those who encourage violence in the name of animal activism. My family and I have been the targets of death threats, as have many of my colleagues. Several animal extremist organizations have been identified by the FBI as serious domestic terrorism threats.

A publicly available report from the FBI describes People for the Ethical Treatment of Animals as an organization that 'recruits interns for the sole purpose of committing criminal acts'.

In 2003, a representative of the Physicians' Committee for Responsible Medicine, another national group that has been prominent in the local debate, called for the assassination of doctors whose research involves animals.

Fortunately, very few people endorse such extreme views. Surveys show that most Americans support the need for animal studies aimed at medical advances. Even as divergent as the views of animal activists and researchers may seem to be, there is agreement on one key issue: we all look forward to a day when mankind's ingenuity provides a way to completely eliminate the need for animal studies.

I have a challenge to offer anyone who feels strongly about this topic, especially young people. If you sincerely wish to eliminate the need for animal research, put down your picket signs, learn about the subject and invent solutions. I guarantee you'll find a receptive audience in the medical research community, because it's a goal we share.

Dr George Poste is a veterinarian and director of the Biodesign Institute at Arizona State University.

www.azcentral.com

What's wrong with testing on animals?

Every year, millions of animals are poisoned, blinded, and killed in crude tests to evaluate the toxicity of consumer products and their ingredients. Rats, mice, guinea pigs, rabbits, and other animals are forced to swallow or inhale huge quantities of a test substance or endure the pain of a chemical eating away at their sensitive eyes and skin.

But the suffering and death of these animals is entirely unnecessary in the making of products like your shampoo, eye shadow, and toilet cleaner. No law requires animal testing of cosmetics or personal care and household cleaning products, so manufacturers of these products have no excuse for inflicting suffering on animals. Companies that test these types of products on animals should be boycotted until they change to a non-animal-testing policy.

You may think companies that test on animals do so for your safety, but these tests usually aren't reliable in determining a chemical's effect on humans. Reactions can vary greatly from species to species so it is quite difficult to come to any conclusions about what a substance will do to humans by testing it on a rabbit. In fact, animal tests also tend to be more expensive than alternative methods, making them both unkind and inefficient.

Many of the companies that manufacture cosmetics and household products have turned their backs on animal testing in favour of the various non-animal test methods available today. These include human

➜

cell cultures and tissue studies (in vitro tests) and artificial human 'skin' and 'eyes' that mimic the body's natural properties, and a number of computer virtual organs that serve as accurate models of human body parts. One example is EPISKIN™ and EpiDerm™, multi-layered skin models made up of cultures of human skin cells, which have been scientifically validated and accepted around the world as total replacements for rabbit skin corrosion studies.

The best way to pressure companies to give up animal testing is to boycott their products.

Alternatives to animal testing

Testing without torture

Besides saving countless animal lives, alternatives to animal tests are efficient and reliable. Unlike crude, archaic animal tests, non-animal methods usually take less time to complete, cost only a fraction of what the animal experiments they replace cost, and are not plagued with species differences that make extrapolation difficult or impossible. Effective, affordable, and humane research methods include studies of human populations, volunteers, and patients, as well as sophisticated in vitro, genomic, and computer-modelling techniques.

Forward-thinking companies are exploring modern alternatives. For example, Pharmagene Laboratories, based in Royston, England, is the first company to use only human tissues and sophisticated computer technologies in the process of drug development and testing. With tools from molecular biology, biochemistry, and analytical pharmacology, Pharmagene conducts extensive studies of human genes and how drugs affect those genes or the proteins they make. While some companies have used animal tissues for this purpose, Pharmagene scientists believe that the discovery process is much more efficient with human tissues. 'If you have information on human genes, what's the point of going back to animals?' says Pharmagene cofounder Gordon Baxter.

Global Action Network, www.gan.ca

Animal testing: science or fiction?

MPs, medical professionals and scientists unite in demanding a thorough evaluation of the utility of vivisection

By Kathy Archibald

The Ecologist Online

Most of us know that cancer, heart disease and stroke are the leading causes of death in the West. But many people would be surprised by the next biggest killer: side effects of prescription medicines. Adverse drug reactions kill more than 10,000 people a year in the UK (and more than 100,000 in the US), costing the NHS alone £466m per year.

The pharmaceutical establishment constantly reassures us that all drugs are tested for safety and efficacy on animals before they can be administered to humans. When challenged about the ethics of vivisection, their defence typically goes like this: 'Which do you think is more important: your child's life or a rat's?' Given the choice most people would thankfully sacrifice the rat.

But what if you were told that the current animal testing procedures are seriously flawed? Consider the following evidence:

Arthritis drug Vioxx, withdrawn from the global market in September 2004, appeared to be safe and even beneficial to the heart in animals, but caused as many as 140,000 heart attacks and strokes in the US alone. The associate safety director of the US Food and Drug Administration (FDA) described it as the 'single greatest drug-safety catastrophe in the history of the world'.

Many studies published in the scientific literature comparing drug side effects in humans and animals have found animal tests to be less predictive than tossing a coin. One review of human–animal correlation in drugs that had been withdrawn because of adverse reactions found that animal tests predicted the human side effects only six out of 114 times.

Hundreds of drugs to treat strokes have been found safe and effective in animal studies and then injured or killed patients in clinical trials.

Hormone-replacement therapy (HRT), prescribed to many millions of women because it lowered monkeys' risk of heart disease and stroke, *increases* women's risks of these conditions significantly. The chairman of the German Commission on the Safety of Medicines described HRT as 'the new thalidomide'. In August 2003 *The Lancet* estimated that HRT had caused 20,000 cases of breast cancer over the past decade in Britain, in addition to many thousands of heart attacks and strokes.

Dr Richard Klausner, former director of the US National Cancer Institute (NCI), lamented: 'The history of cancer research has been a history of curing cancer in the mouse. We have cured mice of cancer for decades, and it simply didn't work in humans.' The NCI also believes we have *lost* cures for cancer because they were ineffective in mice.

Cigarette smoke, asbestos, arsenic, benzene, alcohol and glass fibres are all safe to ingest, according to animal studies.

Of 22 drugs shown to have been therapeutic in spinal cord injury in animals, not one is effective in humans.

Of 20 compounds known not to cause cancer in humans, 19 do cause cancer in rodents.

Dr Albert Sabin, the inventor of the polio vaccine, swore under oath that the vaccine 'was long delayed by the erroneous conception of the nature of the human disease based on misleading experimental models of [it] in monkeys'.

Penicillin, the world's first antibiotic, was delayed for more than 10 years by misleading results from experiments in rabbits, and would have been shelved for ever had it been tested on guinea pigs, which it kills. Sir Alexander Fleming himself said: 'How fortunate we didn't have these animal tests in the 1940s, for penicillin would probably never have been granted a licence, and possibly the whole field of antibiotics might never have been realised.'

Even the Handbook of Laboratory Animal Science admits that 'uncritical reliance on the results of animal tests can be dangerously misleading and has cost the health and lives of tens of thousands of humans'.

So why use animals to test new drugs?

The UK Medicines Act was implemented to ensure that the FDA received proof of safety and efficacy for all new drugs. The intention was good but the reliance placed on animal tests to ensure safety was tragically ill-informed.

It has been known among scientists and the pharmaceutical industry for decades that animal testing is scientifically unreliable. As long ago as September 1962 *The Lancet* commented: 'We must face the fact that the most careful tests of a new drug's effects on animals may tell us little of its effect in humans.' In 1964 Dr J Gallagher, the medical director of Lederle Laboratories, admitted: 'Animal studies are done for legal reasons and not for scientific reasons.'

So, pharmaceutical companies conduct animal tests simply to satisfy government regulators. Crucially, animal data also provide liability protection when drugs kill or injure people. Industry can point to the rigorous animal tests they have performed and claim that they have done their best to ensure against tragedies occurring, thus minimising any damages awarded against them.

From the perspective of satisfying the regulators, pragmatic selection of species will demonstrate whatever is required of a drug, whether it is →

favourable safety or efficacy. And companies are not required to submit all their animal data, but only that from any two species (one rodent and one higher mammal). Dr Irwin Bross, former director of the world's largest cancer research institute, the Sloan-Kettering, observed: 'Whenever government agencies or polluting corporations want to cover up an environmental hazard, they can always find an animal study to "prove" their claim. They can even do a new animal study which will come out the way they want by choosing the "right" animal model system.'

Placing massive emphasis on animal-safety data has also allowed pharmaceutical companies to avoid the expense of conducting clinical trials as extensively as they should. Since the 1950s doctors have been saying that clinical trials should involve more people, last for a longer period of time and use representatives of a broader swathe of society than the young, white males of standard practice. Women are generally not utilised in case they might be pregnant: the manufacturer would be held liable for any unanticipated birth defects. Very often trials do not even include representatives of the patient population the drug is designed to treat. This absurd situation clearly needs to be addressed.

There is no getting away from the fact that people have to be the ultimate guinea pigs for testing new treatments. Clearly, the health and safety of research volunteers and patients should be paramount and the best safeguards should be in place to protect them.

Testing drugs safely on people

New drugs go through three basic testing phases: in vitro (test tube) and in silico (computer) modelling; animal testing; and, finally, human trials.

Before a drug is tested in humans, there should be persuasive evidence that it is safe and effective. No method, neither animal, human nor test-tube, can predict the reactions of every patient with 100 per cent accuracy. Reactions differ between sexes, ages, ethnic groups, even between family members. We are all different, but not as different from each other as we are from animals, with which the differences are so great that they render extrapolation hazardous. Non-animal methods are not completely fail-safe, but do offer more security. There are excellent in silico and in vitro testing methods available today. Many companies specialise in virtual screening of drugs for potentially toxic effects. A wide range of predictive software is available, including complete clinical trial simulations. Other companies focus on safety and efficacy assessments in human tissues. A 10-year international study proved that human cell culture tests are more accurate and yield more useful information about toxic mechanisms than traditional animal tests.

In place of animal-based pre-clinical studies, subsequent clinical trial patients and volunteers would be better protected by the adoption of preliminary microdosing studies (or 'phase 0' clinical trials). Microdose studies involve the administration of ultra-small (and safe) doses of the test drug to volunteers monitored by scanners.

Human microdosing, based on the concept that the best model for man is man, helps in selecting the best drug candidates before advancing into full development, thereby reducing the chances of failure in later, more risky and more expensive phases.

During clinical trials, relevant pharmacological measurements should be made, which would give early warning of potential problems. It is true that some rare side effects will only be detected when drugs are prescribed to large numbers of people. This is why post-marketing drug surveillance is so important and should be strengthened, in order to pick up these effects as quickly as possible. Reports of adverse reactions to drugs are currently soaring in the US, where a record 422,500 adverse events were reported to the FDA in 2004. The FDA cautions that the actual number is likely to be between 10 and 100 times greater because of under-reporting.

Substantial evidence exists that animal tests are inadequate for the task they are supposed to perform, but, incredibly, this has never been systematically investigated. The *only* responsible course of action is to evaluate animal testing scientifically, in an *independent* and *transparent* manner.

By Kathy Archibald Director of Europeans for Medical Progress

www.theecologist.co.uk

5 PERSONAL WRITING

Reading personal writing

Personal writing covers a wide range of topics and genres. It comprises any type of writing in which a writer sets out to share his or her own experiences, opinions or impressions with a reader. The writer's main intention is to recreate the experience being described, usually in an informal way so that the readers feel that they are being taken into the writer's confidence. Because of the very wide range of topics and experiences which can be communicated in this way, it is difficult and not necessary to categorise precisely the different types of personal writing; however, genres such as autobiography, travel writing and reflective essays are some of the most common.

We have, in fact, already looked at some examples of personal writing in earlier chapters, particularly in Chapters 3 and 4, but in these examples we were considering the ways in which the writers either produced a *description* of something or how they *presented an argument*. In the section that follows, we will look at personal writing in a more specific way to consider how writers present themselves and their own particular experiences to the reader and, in particular, how accounts of an individual's experiences can be made relevant and of interest to an audience who have no personal acquaintance with the writer.

Here are three examples of personal writing. All of them are autobiographical in approach and all of them are concerned with the writer's childhood experiences of education and school. All three writers have different experiences and come from different cultures and generations. Although their individual circumstances differ from each other and, almost certainly, differ from those of their readers, the insecurities they experienced, nevertheless, allow their readers to relate to similar emotions they may have had in their own early days at school.

- Martha Jean Baker was at school in the USA in the period immediately after the Second World War.
- The Sri Lankan-born television presenter, George Alagiah, recounts his initial experiences after leaving Ghana, where his family were living, to attend a boarding school in the UK in the late 1960s.
- The poet Laurie Lee describes his first day at school in an English country village in the period following the First World War.

Read the passages carefully and then answer the questions that follow.

Passage 1

Unfriendly teachers and students made early schooldays a misery for Martha Jean Baker. After a mishap with a Christmas tree she was left frightened and humiliated by the school principal. But she was to get her revenge ...

1 It comes back to me every year at this time. As beautifully decorated Christmas trees fill most homes and public spaces, I am overcome by a mixture of admiration and apprehension. A week or two ago, as my partner and I took a short break in London, I was confronted by a large tree in the lobby of our smart hotel. I made sure I never got too close to it. It's been that way for almost 60 years.

2 My childhood was carefree until I started at Douglas school in Minneapolis. There are pictures of me as a smiling, bright-looking little thing. I remember people telling me how cute and clever I was as my older sister took me up and down the street where we first lived in the city. The only worries I can remember were about my hair: if it couldn't be beautiful and straight and red like my sister's, then why couldn't my curls at least fall in neat, dark ringlets?

3 In October 1949, not long after I turned five, my father left his job with food manufacturer General Mills. I may have felt some sadness at the news, since that job had given me the opportunity to meet the Lone Ranger, whose TV show was sponsored by the company. We moved from a four-room apartment to a big house, and then my father started his own chemical business, working from home for a few years. My sister and I entered Douglas school where we were the only Jewish family.

4 Right from the beginning, I felt different. In my memory, at least, the other little girls were mostly blonde with straight hair and clear, pale complexions, while I had very curly dark brown hair and a face covered with freckles. They wore short, pert dresses in bright colours; I had hand-me-downs from my sister, who was three years older than me and big for her age, or from the children of my parents' friends. They were always too long, falling well below my knees.

5 At school, there would be birthday parties where the entire class, so it seemed to me, would march off at lunchtime to someone's house for a party. Inevitably the hostess would tell me, 'I'm having a birthday party and we're going to have peaches with faces on them', but, 'My parents won't let me play with you.'

6 My teacher also made fun of me, of my backward clothes and what she saw as my unkempt hair, and brought me to tears by telling everyone that I talked too much. It is true that I came from a family where curiosity was encouraged, and my sister and I were rarely banished from adult company, except when there was a serious political meeting going on. We could sit on the stairs and listen, or sneak into the kitchen, if we were quiet.

7 I never learned to be one of those shy, quiet little girls, but before I started at Douglas school I always felt loved and happy in the world. When I think back, that teacher set the example for the other children. Sometimes, when she wrote something on the blackboard and told us, 'This says ...' I would interrupt and say, 'No it doesn't! It says ...' She did not like that and would punish me in front of my classmates by making fun of me. Often she would make me sit alone and prevent me from playing with the other girls and boys.

8 At the end of the year the school put up a huge, lavishly decorated Christmas tree near the entrance, right outside the principal's office. There was a real atmosphere of excitement in the school, and I shared the feelings of most of the children. I used to look at beautiful trees and try to imagine what it would be like to have one. This was almost as good as having one at home.

9 That part of America is known for its hot summers and freezing winters. By December it was very cold, and all the children wrapped up for the walk to and from school. One day, shortly after the tree went up, I was standing admiring it when I turned suddenly, probably to start my walk home. My heavy, full coat and long scarf swung around with me and brushed against the tree.

10 I heard a crash and the sound of breaking glass as one of the ornaments was knocked to the ground. The principal heard the sound too. She ran up to me, grabbed me by the arm and marched me into her office. I was terrified. Everyone knew that only 'bad children' were taken to the principal's office, and then they were punished in ways we could only imagine. She told me I had done a terrible and careless thing, and ended by saying, 'You must go home and tell your parents, and take an ornament off your own tree and bring it to replace the one you broke. If you don't, I will contact your parents, and then you'll see...' I was in tears all the way home.

11 I didn't dare tell my parents what had happened; I did not have an ornament I could bring from home, even secretly. My sister and I were probably the only children in the school who did not have a tree of our own.

12 I kept imagining what punishment the principal would find for me, and how my teacher would continue it. Would she hit me? Would she make the other children hate me more and make me cry again? Would she make me sit alone while the others did fun things such as go on field trips or make butter from cream?

13 I don't know what the principal eventually told my parents, and I don't think I ever was punished in the ways I feared. Yet I was left frightened and humiliated. The whole horrible business also reinforced my feeling of difference, of being set apart from the other children. I didn't dare go near that tree again, or the ones that followed it in later years. The other children would stop me from even looking at it, I thought. Everyone knew!

14 Even now, however, I am consoled by the thought that none of this entirely broke my spirit. As I got older, I learned that it was the custom in our school that if a child gave a teacher or the principal flowers she would keep them on her desk for at least the rest of the day. Our house had lilac bushes in front of it, and when I had a teacher I liked I would break off a branch or two as soon as they were in bloom and bring them to my teacher, who would often keep them on her desk until they wilted. One day another pupil told me that our principal was terribly allergic to a particular kind of white flower that was abundant in our neighbourhood in the springtime. Just the smell of them, I believed, would be enough to make her ill. After that, every year, as soon as the white flowers came into bloom, I would pick a large bunch and present it to the woman who had traumatised me.

The Guardian, Monday, 17 December 2007

Exercise 1

1 Which other word in paragraph 1 most reinforces the apprehension felt by the writer when she sees a Christmas tree?
 a smart
 b confronted
 c decorated
 d close
2 In paragraph 2, the writer tells us that she worried about her hair because it was:
 a dark, curly and untidy
 b dark, straight and neat
 c red, neat and curly
 d red, straight and untidy.
3 The writer had met the Lone Ranger because:
 a her father's company financed his programme
 b he gave her father a new job
 c he was an employee of her father's company
 d her father was a friend of his.
4 The clothes the writer wore to school were:
 a brightly coloured
 b three years old
 c too big for her
 d unsuitable for school.
5 The writer's family:
 a had no interest in politics
 b sent their children to bed early
 c thought that children should be seen and not heard
 d treated their children as if they were adults.
6 The Christmas tree put up in the school was:
 a just as the writer had expected
 b big with many decorations
 c like the one the writer had at home
 d outside the school entrance.
7 After breaking the tree ornament the writer cried on her way home because she:
 a did not want to take an ornament from her own tree
 b knew her parents would be angry with her
 c was ashamed of what she had done
 d would not be able to bring in an ornament.
8 The outcome of this experience was that the writer was:
 a afraid to be close to Christmas trees
 b supported by the principal
 c punished by her parents
 d shunned by the other children.
9 The principal of the school attended by the writer:
 a expected the children to bring her flowers
 b had an aversion to a particular type of flower
 c was fond of lilac flowers
 d was the writer's favourite teacher.

10 From what we learn of the writer from this passage we can see that she:
  a did not allow her experience at school to crush her character
  b hated every minute of her time at school
  c never recovered from her experience at school
  d always talked too much at school and at home.

Passage 2

How I became an Englishman

By George Alagiah

As the car stops at the gate, I can see that my father has pulled out his handkerchief. He waves. And then he's gone.

I am alone. I'm not really alone; there are dozens of other boys around me. But I feel lonelier than I have ever felt before. There isn't much else I remember about that day, the day I was dropped off at St John's College.

I do remember my father trying to tip the house prefect who showed us round – an incredibly tall sixth-former called Eilert 'Lofty' Eilertsen – and the rather <u>stilted</u> exchange that followed. But beyond that I cannot remember any detail, just a feeling, an overwhelming sense of displacement.

Perhaps I feel like a woman who's walked into a room full of men: is everyone looking at me or am I just imagining it? I feel awkward; I feel strange. Suddenly my voice doesn't seem right, even the 'English' accent that I thought I had perfected. I feel different.

Above all, I feel foreign. It was the moment I realised I was going to have to develop a pretty thick skin if I was going to make it in England.

The list of things I had to get used to range from the <u>culinary</u> to the comical. There was food that tasted as if it had been brought to the table before the cook had had time to put a vital <u>ingredient</u> in it (to me, even the breakfast Weetabix were strange, like bricks made out of sawdust) and the loo seats that made you jump because they were so cold.

For quite a while I took to lining the seat with sheets of toilet paper. It was a terribly delicate operation and took me so long that eventually I abandoned the practice and resigned myself to the sharp shock treatment.

Virtually everything I did, I was doing for the first time. There were new clothes, new friends, new habits, new lessons and a strange new vocabulary to get used to.

Exercise 2

1. Which two things does George Alagiah describe that he found particularly strange in his first days at school in England? Give some detail in your own words for each one.
2. In the last paragraph on page 75, how does George emphasise the strangeness of everything?

Perhaps the biggest challenge was pronunciation. The first casualty in this department was my name.

It took just a couple of morning registrations to realise that attempts to cling on to the Tamil way of pronouncing Alagiah were futile. The way we used to say it, the way it was meant to be said, the 'al' is more like the beginning of Ullswater and the 'g' is more like an 'h'. So phonetically you might write it as 'Ullerhiya'. Simple really.

But not if you were Mr 'Wally-Whiff' Walsworth of class IW. The 'whiff' in question was the stale afterburn of a packet of Woodbine cigarettes a day. It seemed easier to let him mispronounce the name than to hear him mangle it in a vain and embarrassing attempt to get it right. Looking back, it was me who was embarrassed, not him. In those days, before anyone was really talking about diversity or multiculturalism, you felt like apologising if you had a 'funny' name.

But it wasn't just names. English, as spoken by the English, is full of verbal pitfalls which only the most alert and watchful foreigner avoids. There are two particular areas that gave me trouble.

The first was where to put the stress in a multi-syllable word. Take the word *simplicity*. In Ghana, if we ever used it, we would have split it in two at a convenient point and come out with simply-city, with a more or less equal stress on the two parts. At St John's that would have been greeted with howls of derision, with some joker mimicking me for the rest of the day. So I learned to place the stress where most English people put it, as in sim-**plic**-ity.

I say that's the way most English say it, because even the English are not always agreed on exactly where the stress should be on some words. You will hear some people talk about a contro-versy and others talk about a con-**trov**-ersy. If the locals can't agree, what hope was there for a 12-year-old foreign boy?

The other difficulty was with certain letters, the main culprits being v and w, especially when they were in close proximity. Every time somebody asked me how I was getting on, I had to make a conscious effort not to say I was doing 'wery vell, thank you'. Even now, as a presenter on the nation's most watched news programme, I am careful to rearrange my v-words and w-words lest some atavistic urge to mix them up breaks through. Imagine how I felt, back in February 2005, when I had to tell a TV audience of millions that Charles and Camilla had changed their 'Windsor wedding venue' from the castle to the town hall!

And then there is the question of accent. In Ghana, I had adopted the quasi-pidgin style that we all used in the playground. We used to say 'socca' not soccer; I had 'sistahs' not sisters; I showed 'respec' to my teachers. At home, I spoke like my parents, with an Asian lilt.

So how, after arriving in England, did I end up with the middle-class, southern counties accent you hear when I read the news? It certainly didn't come from my schoolmates, most of whom spoke with the local Portsmouth twang. Nor did I choose it in any conscious way; instead, I grew into it. It's as if, as a child immigrant, I had a built-in instinct which helped me to tune into the one accent that would enable ready acceptance into English society.

Exercise 3

3 Why was the teacher of class 1W given his nickname?

4 Why was George embarrassed when Mr Walsworth mispronounced his name? What does he imply about the teacher?

5 What was the problem George faced in February 2005 when he was reading the news about the wedding of Charles and Camilla? What does he mean by an 'atavistic urge'?

6 How many different accents did George speak in before he came to England? What were they? How did he change his way of speaking when he was in England? Explain, using your own words, what benefit he gained from speaking in this way.

Extension task

7 George talks about having problems knowing where to put the stress on English multi-syllable words. Do you know the rule for stress that is used with 'simplicity'? If not, ask your teacher or look it up. Give some other examples of words that follow the rule. Can you think of other exceptions like 'controversy'?

Ready acceptance by most, that is. One dark winter's evening, a friend and I were walking back towards the college after a trip to the fish and chip shop.

We were aware of a group of skinheads behind us and attempted to do what only genuine hard men pull off, look tough and unruffled even from behind. We failed miserably, largely because we were not at all hard and we were scared witless.

First came the taunts.

'Getting scared, are we? Come on, let's have a look at you.'

➜

And then we heard the sound of breaking glass. It had the same sort of effect as a starting gun at the Olympics, except that in our case it was not adrenalin, but pure, undiluted fear that kicked in.

We sprinted. We were both on the school's 100-metre team, and I reckon we broke a record or two that evening.

Back in college we had a story to tell. And the way we told it, it was a close-run thing, a near miss with the forces of evil. That's how I dealt with the incident in public.

Alone in bed, later that evening, it was different. I knew I had learned something about this country which I had not really been prepared for. I'm not sure that the word racism entered my head, but I understood from that day on that there was an ugliness in British society and that I might see it more often than most simply because of what I looked like and where I came from.

Those skinhead taunts introduced a splinter of fear that niggled away for years to come. But I'm not going to pretend that I was a victim of racism in the way that countless others were at the time and thousands are today. At boarding school I lived in splendid isolation. For every time that I was subjected to racist abuse – there was the occasional abuse on the sports field and even the odd snide remark in the classroom – I can remember many more times when my colour simply did not matter.

Or, if it was remarked upon at all, it was in what I think was an endearing way. Occasionally, one of my friends would call me 'black magic', a pun on a brand of chocolate popular at the time. Far from trying to belittle me, they were, in an admittedly gauche way, trying to show how at ease they were with my colour. I was happy to judge people by what they meant to do rather than what they appeared to do.

What happened to me at school amounted to a kind of total immersion therapy: sink or swim. One day you're in Africa, the next you're in England. One day your parents are there for you, the next they are thousands of miles away. One day you're a foreigner, the next you have to learn to be English. It's all or nothing.

Exercise 4

8 When George and his friend became aware of the group of skinheads, why did they at first attempt to look 'tough and unruffled'? In your own words, give two reasons why they did not succeed.
9 What do you think they were afraid of when they heard the sound of breaking glass?
10 How did they succeed in getting out of trouble?
11 Why was the incident particularly significant for George?
12 If you need to, look up the meaning of 'gauche'. Then explain in your own words why George describes his nickname of 'black magic' as 'gauche'. Why was he not offended by it?

13 In the last paragraph, George says that being sent to an English boarding school was a 'kind of total immersion therapy'. Using the information in the rest of the paragraph, (a) give the three-word phrase that explains the image, and (b) explain one of the examples he uses. Why is this image effective?

From the whole passage

14 For each of the words underlined in the passage, choose the option (**A**, **B**, **C**, or **D**) that has the same meaning that the word has in the passage.

a **stilted**

A formal **B** awkward **C** forced **D** pompous

b **culinary**

A digestible **B** palatable **C** nutritious **D** dietary

c **ingredient**

A additive **B** factor **C** constituent **D** part

d **mangle**

A distort **B** destroy **C** spoil **D** tarnish

e **conscious**

A definitive **B** deliberate **C** painstaking **D** careful

f **snide**

A provoking **B** hateful **C** spiteful **D** annoying

15 Looking back over the whole passage, what qualities do you think George possessed which enabled him to fit in at school and become a success in English society? Find an example for each quality you list.

Passage 3

From *Cider with Rosie* by Laurie Lee

The village school at that time provided all the instruction we were likely to ask for. It was a small stone barn divided by a wooden partition into two rooms – The Infants and The Big Ones. There was one dame teacher, and perhaps a young girl assistant. Every child in the valley crowding there, remained till he was fourteen years old, then was presented to the working field or factory with nothing in his head more burdensome than a few mnemonics, a jumbled list of wars, and a dreamy image of the world's geography. It seemed enough to get by with, in any case; and was one up on our poor old grandparents.

This school, when I came to it, was at its peak. Universal education and unusual fertility had packed it to the walls with pupils. Wild boys and girls from miles around – from the outlying farms and half-hidden hovels way up at the ends of the valley – swept down each day to add to our numbers, bringing with them strange oaths and odours, quaint garments

→

and curious pies. They were my first amazed vision of any world outside the womanly warmth of my family; I didn't expect to survive it for long, and I was confronted with it at the age of four.

★★★★★

The morning came, without any warning, when my sisters surrounded me, wrapped me in scarves, tied up my bootlaces, thrust a cap on my head, and stuffed a baked potato in my pocket.

'What's this?' I said.

'You're starting school today.'

'I ain't. I'm stopping 'ome.'

'Now, come on, Loll. You're a big boy now.'

'I ain't.'

'You are.'

'Boo-hoo.'

They picked me up bodily, kicking and bawling, and carried me up to the road.

'Boys who don't go to school get put into boxes, and turn into rabbits, and get chopped up Sundays.'

I felt this was overdoing it rather, but I said no more after that.

I arrived at the school just three feet tall and fatly wrapped in my scarves. The playground roared like a rodeo, and the potato burned through my thigh. Old boots, ragged stockings, torn trousers and skirts, went skating and skidding around me. The rabble closed in; I was encircled; grit flew in my face like shrapnel. Tall girls with frizzled hair, and huge boys with sharp elbows, began to prod me with hideous interest. They plucked at my scarves, spun me round like a top, screwed my nose, and stole my potato.

★★★★★

I was rescued at last by a gracious lady – the sixteen-year-old junior-teacher – who boxed a few ears and dried my face and led me off to The Infants. I spent that first day picking holes in paper, then went home in a smouldering temper.

'What's the matter, Loll? Didn't he like it at school, then?'

'They never gave me the present!'

'Present? What present?'

'They said they'd give me a present.'

> 'Well, now, I'm sure they didn't.'
>
> 'They did! They said: "You're Laurie Lee, ain't you? Well, just you sit there for the present." I sat there all day but I never got it. I ain't going back there again!'
>
> But after a week I felt like a veteran and grew as ruthless as anyone else. Somebody had stolen my baked potato, so I swiped somebody else's apple. The Infant Room was packed with toys such as I'd never seen before – coloured shapes and rolls of clay, stuffed birds and men to paint. Also a frame of counting beads which our young teacher played like a harp, leaning her bosom against our faces and guiding our wandering fingers.

Exercise 5

From Section 1

1 Using details from the passage, describe the school that Laurie Lee attended: the building, the children and the subjects they were taught.

2 What were the two reasons for there being so many children attending the school, according to the writer? Use your own words.

3 What did Laurie Lee find strange about the children from the outlying farms and the ends of the valley? How were they different from Laurie Lee's immediate family?

4 Explain, using your own words:
- a 'nothing in his head more burdensome than a few mnemonics'
- b 'a dreamy image of the world's geography'
- c 'half-hidden hovels'
- d 'quaint garments'.

From Section 2

5 Why does the writer use direct speech at this point? How does the writer's language convey Loll's thoughts and feelings?

6 The writer uses a completely different technique to describe the activity of the school playground. What is it and how is it effective?

From Section 3

7 How did Laurie Lee spend his first day at school? What were his feelings when he reached home?

8 Explain, using your own words, Laurie Lee's misunderstanding about 'the present'.

9 How did Laurie Lee's feelings towards school change during his first week there?

From the whole passage

10 If you were asked to supply headings for the three sections, what would they be? Do they help you follow the structure of the piece? Would you divide it in different places? Where and why?

11 Lee has written a humorous account of starting school. Select three details which you find amusing and explain why they are so. You should consider how the writer describes the events as well as what happened.

Extension tasks

The following two tasks are more extended than anything you will be asked to write in your examination. But the process of looking at how writers describe similar situations in different ways and the different effects they achieve is a useful one and will help you become more aware of techniques you can use yourself. To respond to the tasks, draw on the work you have already done in answering the questions on the individual passages and try to combine it into a coherent whole. You should also find further features to comment on.

1 Both Martha Jean Baker and George Alagiah describe their experiences of being outsiders in their schools. Write a detailed comparison of their accounts. In particular you should write about the situations they describe, the ways in which they dealt with them and the words and phrases that they use.
2 All three passages are written by adults looking back at their school days. By referring closely to all three passages, comment on how you think their school experience helped to shape their characters in later life.

Further reading exercises on personal writing

Passage 4

From *The Life and Times of the Thunderbolt Kid*

The city of Des Moines's greatest commercial institution was Younker Brothers, the principal department store downtown. Younkers was enormous. It occupied two buildings, separated at ground level by a public alley, making it the only department store I've ever known, possibly the only one in existence, where you could be run over while going from menswear to cosmetics. Younkers had an additional outpost across the street, known as the Store for Homes, which housed its furniture departments and which could be reached by means of an underground passageway beneath Eighth Street, via the white goods department. I've no idea why, but it was immensely satisfying to enter Younkers from the east side of Eighth and emerge a short while later, shopping completed, on the western side. People from out in the state used to come in specially to walk the passageway and to come out across the street and say, 'Hey. Whoa. Golly.'

Younkers was the most elegant, up to the minute, briskly efficient, satisfyingly <u>urbane</u> place in Iowa. It employed twelve hundred people. It had the state's first escalators – 'electric stairways' they were called in the early days – and first air conditioning. Everything about it – its silkily swift revolving doors, its gliding stairs, its whispering elevators, each with its own white-gloved operator – seemed designed to pull you in and keep you happily, contentedly consuming. Younkers was so vast and wonderfully rambling that you seldom met anyone who really knew it all. The book department inhabited a shadowy, secretive balcony area, reached by a pokey set of stairs, that made it cosy and club-like – a place known only to aficionados. It was an outstanding book department, but you can meet people who grew up in Des Moines in the 1950s who had no idea that Younkers *had* a book department.

But its *sanctum sanctorum* was the Tea Room, a place where doting mothers took their daughters for a touch of elegance while shopping. Nothing about the Tea Room remotely interested me until I learned of a ritual that my sister mentioned in passing. It appeared that young visitors were invited to reach into a wooden box containing small gifts, each beautifully wrapped in white tissue and tied with ribbon, and select one to take away as a permanent memento of the occasion. Once my sister passed on to me a present she had acquired and didn't much care for – a die-cast coach and horses. It was only two and a half inches long, but exquisite in its detailing. The doors opened. The wheels turned. A tiny driver held thin metal reins. The whole thing had obviously been hand-painted. I had never seen, much less owned, such a fine thing before.

From time to time after that for years I besought them to take me with them when they went to the Tea Room, but they always responded vaguely that they didn't like the Tea Room so much any more or that they had too much shopping to do to stop for lunch. (Only years later did I discover that in fact they went every week; it was one of those secret womanly things moms and daughters did together.) But finally there came a day when I was perhaps eight or nine that I was shopping downtown with my mom, with my sister not there, and my mother said to me, 'Shall we go to the Tea Room?'

I don't believe I have ever been so eager to accept an invitation. We ascended in an elevator to a floor I didn't even know Younkers had. The Tea Room was the most elegant place I had ever been – like a state room from Buckingham Palace magically transported to the Middle West of America. Everything about it was starched and classy and calm. There was light music of a refined nature and the tink of cutlery on china and of ice water carefully poured. I cared nothing for the food, of course. I was waiting only for the moment when I was invited to step up to the toy box and make a selection.

When that moment came, it took me for ever to decide. Every little package looked so perfect and white, so ready to be *enjoyed*. Eventually, I chose an item of middling size and weight, which I dared to shake lightly. Something inside rattled and sounded as if it might be die cast. I took it to my seat and carefully unwrapped it. It

➜

was a miniature doll – an Indian baby in a papoose, beautifully made but patently for a girl. I returned with it and its disturbed packaging to the slightly backward-looking fellow who was in charge of the toy box.

'I seem to have got a *doll*,' I said, with something approaching an ironic chuckle.

He looked at it carefully. 'That's surely a shame because you git one try at the gift box.'

'Yes, but it's a *doll*,' I said. 'For a girl.'

'Then you'll just have to git you a little girl friend to give it to, won'tcha?' he answered and gave me a toothy grin.

Bill Bryson

Exercise 6

1 Why is Younkers called a 'department' store? How many departments are mentioned in the first two paragraphs?
2 Why do you think the writer found it 'immensely satisfying' to enter the store on the east side of Eighth Street and to leave on the west side?
3 Why was the book department particularly appealing?
4 From the first two paragraphs write a summary in which you describe Younkers store as it was when this account was written. Include the buildings and layout, and also the interior features. You should write about 150 words. Use your own words as far as possible.
5 For each of the words or phrases underlined in the passage, choose the option (**A**, **B**, **C**, or **D**) that has the same meaning that the word or phrase has in the passage.
   a **urbane**
      A polite **B** smooth **C** modern **D** sophisticated
   b **consuming**
      A eating **B** purchasing **C** swallowing **D** absorbing
   c **pokey**
      A cramped **B** crowded **C** uncomfortable **D** irregular
   d **touch of elegance**
      A a little polite **B** a bit posh **C** rather refined **D** somewhat cultured
   e **memento**
      A relic **B** souvenir **C** reminder **D** trophy
6 The writer's sister 'didn't much care for' the gift she passed on to him. What was the writer's reaction to it? Give the two phrases which tell the reader this.
7 Why do you think the writer's mother and sister told him that they did not often visit the Tea Room?
8 The writer says that Younkers Tea Room was 'the most elegant place I had ever been'. How does the writer's language in the rest of the paragraph emphasise the elegance? Give at least three details to support your ideas.

9 This passage is intended to be an amusing account of a childhood experience. Explain as fully as you can, how the writer makes it entertaining for the reader. You should consider both the content of the passage and the writer's use of language.

Extension task

Both Bill Bryson and Laurie Lee (Passage 3) describe a time in their childhood. Compare the two passages as fully as you can and in any way you think appropriate.

Passage 5

In this extract from his book *Around the World in 80 Days* Michael Palin, the television presenter and comic actor, describes his experience, in 1988, of travelling by train in China – somewhere he had never been before. N.B. Chairman Mao (Mao Zedong) was Leader of the People's Republic of China from 1949 until his death in 1976.

Up at 6.15. Misty half-light over the Pearl River. To Guangzhou station for the 8.30 train to Shanghai. Through the cycle rush-hour. Only older men still favour Mao jackets. Otherwise it's Western 1950s or, amongst the young, American casual. A Turnerish sunrise spreads over the city, silhouetting the forest of TV aerials turned, despite official discouragement, in the direction of Hong Kong.

The long, elevated motorway to the station is a Western commuter's dream; almost empty at peak travel time. At the station, an immense characterless building in a side square crowned with neon signs advertising Sanyo, Seiko and State Express 555s, there are few vehicles but a huge swell of people. Many are squatting in groups on the main concourse, their baggage consisting of two plastic or string bags, looped around a bamboo pole, and carried on their shoulders. They scan a state-of-the-art dot matrix indicator for news of their train.

Ours is already at the platform, which is clean and well-swept. The eighteen coaches are green and cream painted, of chunky old-fashioned design, ridged along the outside with air vents on top. A stocky girl with a pretty face and a ponytail stands, in the uniform of the railways, at the entrance to our 'Soft Class' coach. Attendants in peaked caps abound (there are fifty to serve this train). One feels that part of China's achievement has been to put as many people as possible into uniform – of any kind.

The 'Hard Class' coaches are already full, their occupants leaning from open windows to buy sandwiches, orange juice and cola, or drinking their tea from big enamel mugs. The 'Intermediate Class' have bunks, but in an open-plan arrangement, and without the homely touches of 'Soft Class' compartments, which include four berths, complete with duvets and fluffy pink cushions, a small table with an embroidered red cloth on

➜

which is set a reproduction oil lamp with cut-glass shade, and, of course, a pot plant. Lace curtains are drawn back at the window.

We leave on time and are quickly out of the city and into a landscape of fields still worked by families with hoes and rakes. Our smiling, ponytailed lady appears with an enormous steaming kettle and fills up my thermos jug. Another attendant follows up with some cups and jasmine tea-bags.

Talk to a helpful railwayman who tells me, among other things, that we have thirteen stops ahead of us on our 35-hour, 1822 kilometre journey. He's called Mr Cha and has worked on the railways for more than twenty years. I ask him, through Mr Xie, one of our minders from China TV, if there were foreigners riding on Chinese railways twenty years ago.

'Oh yes, indeed. But only from countries we were friendly with.'

'Such as?'

'Vietnam, North Korea ...' He can't think of any more names. He gets off at the next stop and leaves me his cap badge as a memento.

At 10.30 plastic bags are brought round to collect our rubbish. Outside, the landscape is still, serene and peaceful. Every stage of rice production is in evidence: planting, growing, harvesting, winnowing and threshing, all non-mechanised, like a series of period tableaux. A couple of perky dogs march across a field, tails in the air.

There is one restaurant car, which appears to exist mainly to service the huge staff, who are to be found in there most times of day, with their caps off, laughing and gossiping. The kitchen is solid and heavy and full of people, with the cooking done by five chefs on cast iron ranges in woks the size of Jodrell Bank. The tablecloths are plastic and two bottles are at each table. I presume they're ornamental as I never see either drunk from by anyone throughout the journey.

Those who don't want the restaurant and haven't brought their own food, can buy carry-on lunches in white polystyrene boxes, which they then throw out of the windows.

At Ganzhou station a wall is being erected at enormous speed, by a workforce consisting of old men, young men, women and boys. Fourteen-year-olds are straining under bamboo yokes from which are suspended pails full of bricks. I counted thirty in one load.

We talk to some of the passengers in Intermediate, including an infectiously enthusiastic lady who has learnt English off the BBC World Service. When asked for an interview she agrees politely and just before we turn over cries, 'Wait a minute!', and rushes off to put on her lipstick.

Mid-afternoon and feeling drowsy as we pass into Hunan province – Mao's province. I talk with Mr Xie, one of our minders from China TV. He's very earnest and calls me 'Mr Mike'.

Now we are in amongst walls of rock rising sheer from the fields, eroded into fantastic shapes. Then we run along a narrow gorge beside a mud brown river, down which stacks of bamboos are being punted. At Zhen-zhou a couple of grimy steam engines stand tantalisingly close to our train. I hop out and ask if I might climb up into the cab. (For train buffs, the engines were 2-10-2s with smoke deflectors, built in 1981.) Whilst in the cab I notice that the engine is parked level with the roof of a long engine shed, roofed with small earthenware tiles, of the kind which one of my friends requested I bring back. Very gently I prise one loose and return to the train, very pleased with myself.

At sunset Swan Lake is playing over the PA as we head out of Hangyang. The chef excels himself and provides the best train meal in 45 days. Pigeon in soy sauce, squid on a hot plate, with tomato, chicken and sea-turtle casserole, fish cutlet, and in the Chinese manner, just as you think the meal is over, soup – in this case cucumber and egg-white. In Intermediate Class they're playing draughts. A lot of people are smoking. The land outside is very dark. The stations we pass through are dismally lit, though large crowds still wait patiently on the platforms.

At Zhuzhou station at 10.15, Dave goes in search of digestive biscuits, a man goes along checking the axle temperature with his bare hands and Mr Xie wants to draw me into conversation about the book I'm reading: *The Horse's Mouth* by Joyce Carey.

'This look very serious book, Mr Mike.'

When I tell him that much of it is raucously funny, he seems very disappointed.

Later, I'm comfortable under the thick duvet but lie awake for quite a while, listening to the ever-changing sounds of the train. It seems wrong to waste any of China in sleep.

Exercise 7

1. In the first two paragraphs, the writer gives many details of the people, the drive to the station and the station itself. List them under two headings 'the old' and 'the new'. Why do you think he chose these particular details to mention?
2. Why do you think the writer and his crew have been given 'minders' by China TV?
3. What is the writer emphasising by including direct speech for Mr Cha?
4. Explain in your own words why Mr Cha leaves the writer his cap badge.
5. How does the writer give the feeling of time passing during the journey? How is this effective?
6. Explain 'like a series of period tableaux'. Why is the image effective? Find three other examples in the passage (one earlier than this and two later) of details that continue this theme.
7. Why does the writer describe the grimy steam engines as '*tantalisingly* close'?

8 For what two reasons do you think the writer is 'very pleased with himself' after the stop at Zhen-zhou?
9 What does the final sentence ('It seems wrong to waste any of China in sleep.') imply about the writer's reaction to his experience in China? Looking back over the whole passage, explain as fully as you can how he communicates this feeling to the reader. You should consider the words and phrases he uses to describe the countryside, the journey itself, and the people he met while travelling.

Writing a personal account

All of the examples of personal writing that we have considered so far in this chapter have been concerned with the writers recounting their responses to a particular incident in their lives. Each piece is written in the **first person** which allows the readers to feel that they are being taken into the confidence of the writer and so they feel immediately engaged.

Four of these pieces of writing are written in the **past tense** and are obviously being recounted many years after the episode(s) being described actually occurred. This approach allows the writers to present the episodes from different perspectives: the children they were at the time the episode happened and the adults they are at the time of writing about the event. For instance, when George Alagiah uses the phrase 'admittedly gauche' to describe his friends, it is a comment from his adult self, not what he would have thought while still a schoolboy. By adopting this approach, the writers are able to present their childhood characters both as someone who is part of themselves but also as someone whom, as adults, they can view with some detachment. This approach allows the readers to appreciate the character of the writer more comprehensively.

Note that George Alagiah starts in the present tense to convey his feelings at the moment his father leaves, and then changes to the past to recount his longer-term experiences at school. This emphasises the strength of his feelings and makes the reader feel them more sharply; they then become the background against which his experiences are set. It is very effective when done as well as this, but it is difficult to pull off so probably best not attempted in the time pressure of an examination.

Michael Palin, on the other hand, writes his account of his journey through China using entirely the **present tense**. This allows him to present his experience in such a way that the reader can imagine that it is actually happening at the same moment as the words are being read. At times, his account reads almost as if it is a diary or a journal. This impression is reinforced by the fact that in places he deliberately writes in non-sentences ('Up at 6.15. Misty half-light over the Pearl River.') to create an impression of immediacy. This is another means by which the reader is engaged.

A further difference between Michael Palin's account and that of the other writers is that he is, perhaps, less interested in presenting the readers with information about his own character than in presenting his impressions of a country and people that he obviously finds very interesting. He comes across to the reader as a reliable and trustworthy observer and because of this, the readers are disposed to share his opinions of the scenery and people that he describes.

The main point that emerges from the previous paragraphs is that when writing a personal account, the key thing to remember is to present your account in such a way that you make yourself both an interesting and trustworthy narrative observer.

Tips for personal writing

Let's look more closely at ways to engage and interest a reader in a piece of personal writing.

Writing a true account

- Remember that as the narrator you are in complete control of what you write. Examination questions are quite often asked in terms of a personal experience, for example: 'Write a story of what happened when you were accused of something you had not done.' Such questions are inviting a narrative told in the first person, with the inclusion of your thoughts, feelings and reactions. It does not have to be true – you may make it up completely, you may base it on something that happened to a friend, or it may have happened to you. What is important is that you make it sound as if it happened to you; that is what the feelings and reactions do. Even Michael Palin, while aiming to be a fairly dispassionate observer, interweaves his reactions – look especially at the adjectives he uses to describe the people he meets. And one important note: *never* write a story in the first person that ends with your death. Think about it: will the reader find it convincing? Why not?
- It is, of course, much easier to write a convincing narrative of something that actually happened to you rather than inventing it from nothing, but even with a true incident it is most unlikely that your readers will have been present when it happened. This means that you have the option of adding or suppressing details as you wish – to allow yourself to craft the account in order to make it more interesting to your readers.
- When you describe an event that is personal to you, it is important that you keep your readers in mind. They will not know the circumstances that led up to the event, the surroundings in which it occurred or the personalities or relationships between any of the characters involved. You must decide how much a reader needs to know in order to gain a full appreciation of the episode about which you are writing. Some scene setting is, therefore, necessary before you start on the main part of your account – but not so much that you overshadow the main incident, or run out of time to do it full justice.
- You must also give some consideration to how you are going to present yourself as a character in the account; for example, are you going to describe the incident exactly as it happened from the point of view of the character you were at the time or will you modify this younger character

by writing about the episode from the perspective of yourself as an older person? The decision is entirely yours.

- You also need to consider how you are going to present the order of events. At what point in the episode should you begin your account? At what point should you conclude it? For example, is it more effective to describe the complete resolution of the event or is it more effective to leave the reader in suspense? Should your account follow closely the sequence of events as they really happened or, in order to make the account more interesting, will it benefit from you re-ordering events, perhaps adding in things that you learnt later, to make them more coherent? Again, the choice is yours as the writer.
- Another point for consideration is how to present other characters who were involved in the event. How much description do you need to include to ensure that they appear as convincing participants rather than just as names on a page? In this type of writing it is important that other characters are given individuality but they should not detract from the central character of the episode which is you, the narrator. Remember that other people's characters can be effectively conveyed by well-chosen examples of what they said and did at particular moments.

Technical skills

Using humour

- Often, the personal experience you choose to write about will be something that would benefit from a humorous treatment. After all, an episode that seemed serious to you at the time it happened may well have become much more amusing now that you look back on it as a more mature person, and you will want to convey this aspect of it to your readers. Humour can be a very effective tool in personal writing if it is handled well. It is, however, something that is not easy to do effectively and you need to think carefully about it.
- Firstly, it is important to decide what was especially funny about the incident you are describing. For example, the humour may be derived from what happened or from what other people said and did. (Note that it is rarely derived from what you yourself said or did!) Another point to consider is whether the intention of your account is to make the reader laugh at something that happened to you or at something you witnessed happening to someone else. The important thing is to have a clear standpoint from which to describe events and to establish characters and setting convincingly so that what is humorous about the account derives naturally from this context.
- Another important point to remember in writing a humorous account is that not everyone laughs at the same thing. You might find the thought of someone falling out of a tree while trying to steal a neighbour's mangoes highly amusing, but someone reading the account may not consider this a funny episode at all! In fact, if you are trying to amuse your readers it is usually more effective to underplay the humour in your writing and to convey humour through the *way* in which your account is written rather than by trying too hard to describe what may well have been funny

events when they happened but which can very easily lose their comedy value when written down in great detail.

The extract from Laurie Lee's autobiography (Passage 3 on pages 79–80) contains an effective example of humorous description. Here it is again:

> The morning came, without any warning, when my sisters surrounded me, wrapped me in scarves, tied up my bootlaces, thrust a cap on my head, and stuffed a baked potato in my pocket.
>
> 'What's this?' I said.
>
> 'You're starting school today.'
>
> 'I ain't. I'm stopping 'ome.'
>
> 'Now, come on, Loll. You're a big boy now.'
>
> 'I ain't.'
>
> 'You are.'
>
> 'Boo-hoo.'
>
> They picked me up bodily, kicking and bawling, and carried me up to the road.
>
> 'Boys who don't go to school get put into boxes, and turn into rabbits, and get chopped up Sundays.'
>
> I felt this was overdoing it rather, but I said no more after that.

What makes this a humorous piece of writing? Firstly, the writer presents the experience very much from within the limited consciousness of himself as a young child. Because of the context within the narrative, the reader easily guesses what is going to happen, but the child is unsure. His choice of verbs to describe events in the first paragraph of the extract (*surrounded*, *wrapped*, *tied up*, *thrust*, *stuffed*) all suggest aggressive actions and help to present a picture of an innocent child being dominated by the much more powerful forces which are his sisters. Added to this is the apparently incongruous and mysterious action of filling his pocket with something as unexpected as a baked potato.

This descriptive paragraph is then followed by a burst of dialogue that gains particular force from the fact that words identifying who is saying what are kept to the minimum. The writer does not tell his readers that they should be laughing here – he simply presents the occasion and lets it speak for itself. As the extract goes on, the narrator's protests become increasingly ineffectual until he collapses into tears (*Boo-hoo*).

Next comes the comic description of the bawling child being carried bodily out of the house and trumped by the sisters' threat that he'll be turned into a rabbit and chopped up and eaten. The whole passage describes something that to the writer at the time it happened must have been quite a terrifying experience. However, in his mature years he has realised that it was only a temporary upset about which he now sees the funny side – which he has successfully conveyed to his readers. His final comment (*I felt this was overdoing it rather*) is a very effective use of understatement for comic effect (litotes).

Using direct speech and dialogue

As mentioned above, one very effective way of producing humour is through the use of direct speech. Quoting the words actually said by somebody, whether for humorous purposes or not, is, in any case, an important feature of personal writing. Again, it needs to be thought about carefully by the writer in order to gain maximum effect. The important point to remember is to be selective in using direct speech and dialogue. Overdoing it can have the result of unnecessarily drawing out the length of your account. Also, it can result in readers losing track of what is being described. The best approach is to select carefully representative examples of what people said and to use them sparingly as Laurie Lee does in the extract above.

Punctuation: direct speech

If you are using direct speech in your writing, it is important that you punctuate it correctly and observe the appropriate conventions. Here are the key points to remember:

- Direct speech should be placed within either double ("…") or single ('…') *inverted commas* (speech marks). It does not matter which form of speech marks you choose to use, but once you have decided, you must be consistent.
- All passages of direct speech must be marked off from the rest of the sentence in which they occur by a comma.
- The opening word of each piece of direct speech must begin with a capital letter.
- You must start a new line for each new speaker.
- If you quote someone else's words within a passage of direct speech then these words must also be enclosed within speech marks. If the original piece of speech is indicated by double inverted commas, then further quotations should be placed within single inverted commas and vice versa.
- If a single piece of direct speech consists of more than one paragraph, then the opening set of inverted commas is repeated at the start of each new paragraph. However, the closing inverted commas are not used until the very end of the passage of speech.

Here are some examples of the three different patterns of direct speech and how they should be punctuated:

1. The teacher said, 'I'm very pleased with the last piece of work you did for me.'
2. 'Thank you, Sir,' I replied, 'but I found it a very difficult assignment. Will we have anything else like that in future?'
3. 'I'm sure you will,' answered the teacher. 'You need as much practice with this topic as you can get.'

In the first example, a comma is used after the introductory verb (*said*) and before the words actually spoken, which begin with a capital letter.

In the second example, the words *I replied* break the direct speech and are separated from the rest of the sentence by commas. The opening word of the second part of this direct speech sentence does not have a capital letter, however, because it continues a sentence that has already begun.

In the final example the two pieces of direct speech, separated by *answered the teacher* are two distinct sentences. The opening word of the second sentence (*You*) is, therefore, given a capital letter.

Punctuation exercise

Punctuate the following passage, putting in paragraphs, commas, full stops, speech marks, capital letters and question marks as necessary.

> the classroom was unusually quiet the principal strode to the front of the room and stood at the teacher's desk he waited for a minute before he spoke i want you all to listen very carefully he said in a quiet voice someone in here has been very rude to a visitor to the school someone shouted the word idiot at the mayor as he walked through the playground i want to know who it was brian raised his hand yes boy said the principal was it you it might have been me sir whispered brian what do you mean it might have been me surely you know if you said it or not brian looked very worried i did call out the word idiot in the playground he said but i didn't see the mayor there he must have thought i was shouting the word at him but all i was doing was shouting at myself we were playing football and i missed an open goal that's the truth sir

Personal writing exercises

1. Write about a time when you were younger when you learnt a lesson from an older person.
2. Write about a place you go to when you want to be alone and why you like to go there.
3. Describe a day at school or at work when things went unexpectedly wrong.
4. Describe your first impressions of a town or country that you visited.
5. Describe your memories of a family gathering that you attended when you were younger.

6 MEDIA TEXTS

Reading media texts

Media texts include advertisements, websites, campaign material and newspaper features. They are produced with a different purpose from argumentative texts or from informative texts, as they are generally written from a promotional standpoint with a bias towards a certain idea or thing. A media text has the intention of persuading its audience to buy what is advertised, to support the writer's campaign or to agree with a particular point of view held by the writer. So, as a reader, you need to bring to media texts the same critical and analytical approach that you bring to any other so-called 'factual' piece of writing.

Some examinations include a media text in their Reading paper, but their use is usually restricted to a short excerpt, a single webpage or a small leaflet. In this chapter we shall be looking at longer examples, but the skills you will be developing are the same as the ones you will need to respond to the shorter pieces.

Media texts tend to use a wide range of techniques to appeal to their readers, the most important of which is the use of pictures, usually in colour. This means that when you are reading a media text you are gaining its meaning not just from the words used by the writer but from the images conveyed by the supporting pictures and other graphical material. The whole item – website, advertisement, leaflet or whatever – is put together to have an effect.

The use of pictures to support a point of view can be very subtle. If the writer of a newspaper article, for example, wants to present an unsympathetic portrayal of someone, then a simple way of reinforcing this impression for the reader is to illustrate the article with an unattractive photograph of the person about whom it is written. For example, a picture of a person frowning, or engaging in an unattractive activity such as chewing his or her fingernails, will present a negative image of that person. On the other hand, a picture of that person smiling or playing with his or her children will present a much more attractive image.

Typically also, the writing in media texts is kept simple in order to have as much impact as possible. Paragraphs are short, sometimes only one sentence, and the way they are arranged on the page is often as important as what they say. Headings and subheadings are used a lot to focus the reader's attention and to point the way through the argument. As with pictures, the precise choice of words for a heading can manipulate the reader's response to the facts presented below it.

For example, the heading 'Cruelty to Animals: Mechanized Madness' (Example 4, page 103) does this very effectively for the following reasons:

1 The three opening words reinforce one of the main points of the article.
2 The alliteration in the phrase 'mechanized madness' places emphasis on the nature of the process being described.
3 The use of bold typeface highlights the content of the section that follows.

When reading media texts it is very important that you consider the overall purpose of the webpage or the leaflet, and keep the writer's likely bias in mind to ensure that you gain as objective an understanding as possible of what is being said and portrayed to you.

Printed below are six media texts; each hopes to encourage its readers to be in favour of what it represents.

- The first two extracts, Examples 1 and 2, are from the websites of World Wide Fund for Nature (WWF) and Friends of the Earth. These organisations are very much concerned with helping to preserve threatened species of animals and also protecting the environment.
- Examples 3 and 4 are extracts from a leaflet published on a website. This was produced by an organisation that supports veganism and wants to convert people to become vegan. The writers of the leaflet present what appears to be a reasoned argument and support it with what appear to be factual details relating to the ways animals are farmed in order to be eaten.
- Examples 5 and 6 are media articles relating to theme parks. They comprise a summary of a scientific survey of the level of dangers in roller coaster rides and a piece of journalism describing a newly opened roller coaster ride.

Read through each example carefully and answer the questions that follow.

Example 1

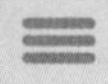

What is Climate Change?

Global warming doesn't mean we'll all have warmer weather in the future.

As the planet heats, climate patterns change, with more extreme and unpredictable weather across the world – many places will be hotter, some colder. Some wetter, others drier.

We know the planet has warmed by an average of nearly 1°C in the past century. Might not sound much, but on a global scale that's a huge increase that's creating big problems for people and wildlife.

Causes of climate change

Over the past 150 years, the world's industrialised nations have changed the balance of the **carbon cycle** by burning huge amounts of fossil fuels (concentrated carbon, like coal, oil, gas), as well as breeding vast numbers of methane-producing livestock, and **cutting down the forests** that naturally absorb carbon dioxide from the air.

The extra carbon in the atmosphere has been raising global temperatures, and the speed of change has been faster than any natural process, and faster than many natural systems can adapt.

Impacts and effects of climate change

Forests

Most people know how vital forests are – they soak up carbon dioxide, the main greenhouse gas responsible for global warming, and help regulate the world's climate. They're also home to countless plant and animal species. We're working with communities, local governments and businesses to ensure the world's forests are protected...

Polar regions

Recent data has shown that Arctic summer sea ice is melting faster than we had expected, and the Intergovernmental Panel on Climate Change has warned that: 'The impacts of climate change in the polar regions over the next 100 years will exceed impacts forecast for other regions, and will have globally significant consequences'.

Animals

For endangered species like the orang-utans in Indonesia and Malaysia – already at risk because of deforestation, habitat loss and illegal hunting – one of the first effects of climate change is likely to be food shortages caused by unusual rainfall patterns. And they're just one of the many species that will be affected...

How WWF is tackling climate change

Getting a global climate deal

Climate change is a global problem – that's why we need international agreement on how to reduce greenhouse gas emissions, conserve forests and help poorer countries adapt to the impacts of a changing climate. We are also working in countries with major economies such as China, India, Brazil, South Africa, the USA and the EU to ensure that they all take ambitious action at home.

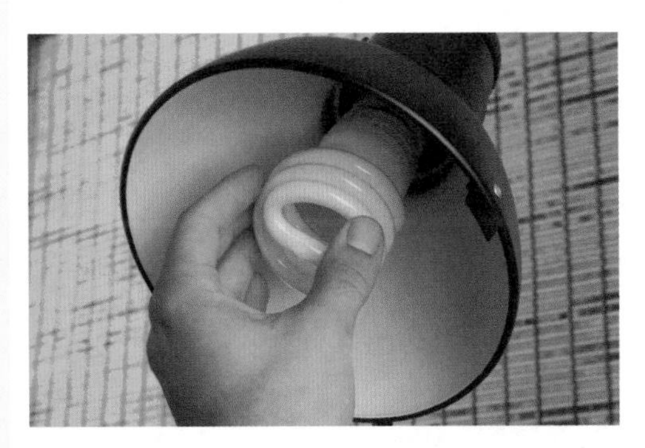

Changing how we live

We're promoting positive changes in the way we all live, to help us live within the capacity of our one, small planet. It's more than just switching to low-energy light bulbs, although that's a positive first step – it's about pushing forward new technologies, climate-smart legislation and greener lifestyles. Take our footprint calculator and help reduce your environmental footprint.

Renewable energy and low-carbon transport

We have a vision for a 100% renewable future by 2050. We're working toward an efficient energy system focused on clean renewable energy sources like wind, wave and solar power.

Transport is another big greenhouse gas emitter. We're particularly focussing on aviation which is one of the fastest growing sources of emissions in the UK. We're persuading companies to reduce business flights and working to secure a global agreement to tackle emissions.

How you can help tackle climate change

Adopt a polar bear

Adopt the Svalbard polar bears and help maintain a healthy Arctic environment.

www.wwf.org.uk

Example 2

Climate Change

Preventing the worst of climate change

Every year we're seeing the impacts of climate change grow. Floods, droughts and storms are all getting worse.

But the world can prevent the worst of climate change. And we'll do this through a massive economic transformation – one that moves the planet off fossil fuels and on to renewable energy.

Exciting changes for the better are already happening. Every day more power from the wind and sun comes on stream. Every day more communities are campaigning to keep fossil fuels in the ground.

The faster we act, the less suffering for people across the planet – from farmers in the Sudan to those hit by flooding in Somerset.

But there's still a long way to go. World **governments lack the ambition** to change at the speed that's needed. And powerful **fossil fuel industries are lobbying** for delays the Earth cannot afford.

We're campaigning with people in the UK and internationally to bring about a **massive energy revolution**, as fast as possible.

We're working on:

- A strong global climate agreement
- Keeping fossil fuels in the ground, including stopping fracking
- Using energy as efficiently and sparingly as possible – it's too precious to waste
- A renewables revolution
- Preparing for the climate change we cannot avoid, like flooding

International climate campaign

Planetary emergency

The **world's leading scientists have given stark warnings** about the planetary emergency we're facing: the impacts of climate change are here and will get worse unless we take immediate action.

You don't have to be a scientist to see the impacts of climate change.

Just after Typhoon Bopha devastated the Philippines last year, Yeb Saño, Head of the Philippines delegation, made an emotional plea at the climate talks in Doha. He said:

Please, no more delays, no more excuses. I ask of all of us here, if not us then who? If not now then when? If not here then where?

We are heading for a **catastrophic temperature rise of 4 degrees Celsius** unless we do something to change it.

A fair, global climate deal

Friends of the Earth is campaigning for a fair global climate deal.

What does that mean? It means **rich countries:**

1 cutting their emissions faster

2 helping developing countries to change over to clean energy.

How much action does each country need to take to stop catastrophic climate change? Find out on our new Climate Fair Shares website.

The UK needs to cut its emissions by **75% by 2030**. But the Government's plans are a long way from achieving this.

Read about the UK's role in a fair, global climate deal.

We must be stronger

Governments are not acting fast enough. We must **unite nationally, regionally and globally** to pressure them to act.

Friends of the Earth is working with others to help build a global climate campaign. Together with our international family, we are pushing for:

- A new Loss and Damage Mechanism to give compensation and redress for countries and communities affected by loss and damage.
- A strengthening of EU emission targets
- Carbon emissions cuts in line with science and justice
- Rich countries to provide finance and technology so that poorer ones can act
- Smart ways to finance the Green Climate Fund – not risky carbon trading schemes
- Clean and affordable energy as a solution to energy poverty
- An immediate ban on all new dirty energy projects including fracking
- Compensation for those affected by climate change

The UK government must do its bit and show leadership by setting science-based targets to decarbonise its own economy.

To keep up to date with our international climate campaign, you can:

- Follow our Campaigner Asad Rehman on twitter @chilledasad100
- Sign up to our International Climate Hub

www.foe.co.uk

Exercise 1

Example 1

1 What does the photograph of the polar bear imply about the species? What is it linked to in the wording below the heading 'What is climate change?'?

2 From the section 'Causes of climate change', state three actions of humans that have led to changes in the world's climate.

3 In the section headed 'Impacts and effects of climate change', the WWF seems to be particularly concerned about protecting forests. Why?

4 In the section headed 'Animals', only one animal that will be affected by climate change is mentioned. Why do you think the orang-utan is singled out? What is the effect of the long phrase inside the two dashes? Does the photograph add to the effect? How?

5 For each of the words or phrases underlined in the passage, choose the option (**A**, **B**, **C**, or **D**) that has the same meaning that the word or phrase has in the passage.

a **unpredictable**

A erratic | **B** unforeseeable | **C** unstable | **D** doubtful

b **global**

A international | **B** universal | **C** comprehensive | **D** worldwide

c **significant consequences**

A serious impacts | **B** important outcomes | **C** powerful influences | **D** noticeable results

d **promoting**

A advertising | **B** encouraging | **C** furthering | **D** upholding

e **legislation**

A laws | **B** controls | **C** orders | **D** mandates

Example 2

6 Read the section of the webpage that appears on page 98. Using your own words, what are the two reasons why climate change is not being tackled as fast as Friends of the Earth would like?

7 In the section headed 'International climate campaign', why is the Friends of the Earth's campaign for a global climate deal called 'fair'? Do you agree? Give your reasons. Where does the website justify the use of the word?

Examples 1 and 2

8 Look again at the other photographs and illustrations used in these websites (that haven't been mentioned in a question yet). Do they all have references in the text? Or do they bring in new ideas of their own? Why another polar bear? Which ones do you think are the most effective in supporting the website's message and encouraging the readers to share the message it is putting across? Why?

9 The websites present a lot of information from different sources, some of it clearly factual and some of it perhaps not. Looking back over both examples, divide the information into two columns, one for 'facts' and

the other 'opinions'. You could subdivide the 'opinions' into those that are ascribed to a stated person and those that seem to be the opinions of the website writers. Is it always clear which is which? What do you think are the reasons for this?

10 Considering your answers to all the questions above, how effective do you think the website material has been in persuading readers to support the views of WWF and Friends of the Earth? In your answer you should consider the content and appearance of the material and the words and phrases it uses.

Example 3

Top Reasons to Go Vegan

Many people's New Year's resolutions include losing weight, eating better, getting healthier, and doing more to make the world a better place. You can accomplish all these goals by switching to a vegan diet, and you'll enjoy delicious, satisfying meals as well. Here are our top reasons to go vegan:

'I am a very strict vegan ... I just really, really love animals, and I act on my values.' – Natalie Portman

1. Slim down while feeling good

Is shedding some extra pounds first on your list of goals for the new year? Vegans are, on average, up to 20 pounds lighter than meat-eaters. And unlike unhealthy fad diets, which leave you feeling tired (and gaining all the weight back eventually), going vegan is the healthy way to keep the excess fat off for good while feeling full of energy.

2. It's the best way to help animals

Every vegan saves more than 100 animals a year from horrible abuse. There is simply no other way that you can easily help so many animals and prevent so much suffering than by choosing vegan foods over meat, eggs, and dairy products.

3. A healthier, happier you

A vegan diet is great for your health! According to the American Dietetic Association, vegans are less likely to develop heart disease, cancer, diabetes, or high blood pressure than meat-eaters. Vegans get all the nutrients they need to be healthy (e.g. plant protein, fiber, minerals, etc.) without all the nasty stuff in meat that slows you down and makes you sick, like cholesterol and saturated animal fat.

4. Vegan food is delicious

So you're worried that if you go vegan, you'll have to give up hamburgers, chicken sandwiches, and ice cream? You won't. As the demand for vegan food skyrockets, companies are coming out with more and more delicious meat and dairy product alternatives that taste like the real thing but are much healthier and don't hurt any animals. Plus, we have thousands of tasty kitchen-tested recipes to help you get started!

➜

5. Meat is gross

It's disgusting but true. Meat is often contaminated with feces, blood, and other bodily fluids, all of which make animal products the top source of food poisoning in the United States. Scientists at the Johns Hopkins Bloomberg School of Public Health tested supermarket chicken flesh and found that 96 percent of the brand tested was contaminated with campylobacter, a dangerous bacterium that causes 2.4 million cases of food poisoning each year, resulting in diarrhea, cramping, abdominal pain, and fever. Learn more.

6. Help feed the world

Eating meat doesn't just hurt animals; it hurts people too. It takes tons of crops and water to raise farmed animals – in fact, it takes up to 16 pounds of grain to produce just 1 pound of animal flesh! All that plant food could be used much more efficiently if it was fed to people directly. The more people who go vegan, the more we can feed the hungry.

7. Save the planet

Eating meat is one of the worst things that you can do for the Earth; it's wasteful, it causes enormous amounts of pollution, and the meat industry is one of the biggest causes of global warming. Adopting a vegan diet is more important than switching to a 'greener' car in the fight against global warming.

8. All the cool kids are doing it

The list of stars who shun animal flesh is basically a 'who's who' of today's hottest celebs. Joaquin Phoenix, Natalie Portman, Ariana Grande, Al Gore, Flo Rida, Tobey Maguire, Shania Twain, Alicia Silverstone, Anthony Kiedis, Casey Affleck, Kristen Bell, Alyssa Milano, Common, Joss Stone, Anne Hathaway, and Carrie Underwood are just some of the famous vegans and vegetarians who regularly appear in *People* magazine.

9. Chickens are smarter than your dog

While most people are less familiar with chickens, fish, and cows than they are with dogs and cats, animals used for food are every bit as intelligent and able to suffer as the animals who share our homes are. Chickens are so smart that their intelligence has been compared by scientists to that of monkeys. Read more about these amazing animals.

Ready to get started? Make 'Go vegan' your New Year's resolution **and we'll help you every step of the way. Have a happy, healthy, and humane new year!**

Exercise 2

1. According to the website material above, why is turning vegan the best way of losing weight?
2. Why should lovers of hamburgers not be concerned about turning vegan?
3. For what reasons do you think the website includes the paragraph headed *Chickens are smarter than your dog*?
4. Write a summary of what you have learned so far about
   - the benefits to people's health of a vegan diet
   - how being vegan can help the Earth and creatures that live on it.

   Use your own words as far as possible and remember to select only relevant points. You should write two paragraphs, one for each bullet point, each of about 110–120 words.

Example 4

Cruelty to Animals: Mechanized Madness

The green pastures and idyllic barnyard scenes of years past are now distant memories. On today's factory farms, animals are crammed by the thousands into filthy windowless sheds, wire cages, gestation crates, and other confinement systems. These animals will never raise their families, root in the soil, build nests, or do anything that is natural to them. They won't even feel the sun on their backs or breathe fresh air until the day they are loaded onto trucks bound for slaughter.

Animals on today's factory farms have very little legal protection from cruelty and often suffer treatment that would be illegal if it were inflicted on dogs or cats: neglect, mutilation, genetic manipulation, and drug regimens that cause chronic pain and crippling, transport through all weather extremes, and gruesome and violent slaughter. Yet farmed animals are no less intelligent or capable of feeling pain than are the dogs and cats we cherish as companions.

The factory farming system of modern agriculture strives to maximize output while minimizing costs. Cows, calves, chickens, turkeys, ducks, geese, and other animals are kept in small cages, in jam-packed sheds, or on filthy feedlots, often with so little space that they can't even turn around or lie down comfortably. They are deprived of exercise so that all their bodies' energy goes toward producing flesh, eggs, or milk for human consumption. The giant corporations that run most factory farms have found that they can make more money by cramming animals into tiny spaces, even though many of the animals get sick and some die. Egg-industry expert Bernard Rollins writes that 'chickens are cheap; cages are expensive'.

Many animals are fed drugs to fatten them faster and to keep them alive in conditions that might otherwise kill them, and many are genetically altered to grow faster or to produce much more milk or eggs than they would naturally. Some animals become crippled under their own weight or die when their heart gives out.

Take a stand against cruelty to animals: **By switching to a vegan diet, you could spare more than 100 animals a year** from this misery. Request a vegan starter kit today!

Turkeys

Ben Franklin called turkeys a 'true original native of America'. He had tremendous respect for their resourcefulness, agility, and beauty.[1] Turkeys are intelligent animals who enjoy having their feathers stroked and listening to music, with which they will often sing quite loudly.[2] In nature, turkeys can fly 55 miles an hour, run 25 miles an hour, and live up to ten years.[3]

But the story's very different for turkeys on factory farms: They will be killed when they are only 5 or 6 months old, and during their short lives, they will be denied even the simplest pleasures, like running, building nests, and raising their young.

Thousands of turkeys are crammed into filthy sheds after their beaks and toes are burned off with a hot blade. Some suffer heart failure or debilitating leg pain,

and they may become crippled under the weight of their genetically manipulated and drugged bodies. When the time comes for slaughter, they are thrown into transport trucks, and when they arrive at the slaughterhouse, their throats are cut and their feathers boiled off – some will still be conscious when this happens.

[1] Benjamin Franklin, "To Mrs. Sarah Bache," 26 Jan. 1784, *The Writings of Benjamin Franklin*, ed. Albert Henry Smyth, New York: The Macmillan Company, 1905–1907.

[2] The Humane Society of the United States, "A First Look at Farm Animals: Turkeys," 2004.

[3] *Ibid.*

Exercise 3

1. What are the 'green pastures and idyllic barnyard scenes' that the writer starts the first paragraph with? What emotions in the reader is the writer intending to arouse? What happens next in the paragraph? What is the effect of this?
2. Look at the second paragraph, where the writer mentions dogs and cats twice. What is the point being made about the differences between the treatment of dogs and cats and other animals? Why is it effective?
3. Why do you think the website includes references as footnotes?
4. List the main arguments the writer makes against factory farming.
5. Example 4 is intended to reinforce the argument to turn vegan in Example 3, in a very persuasive way. Look at the pieces of information given and decide for each whether it is a fact or an opinion. Are there examples of opinions being presented as facts? Do they make the sections more or less persuasive? Why?
6. Now look at the language the writer uses. Write down every word or phrase that you think is emotive, meaning it is designed to arouse an emotional response in the reader. What is the effect if you replace some or all of these with more neutral words? Does that change where you put any of the pieces of information when you were working through Question 5? Why?

Extension task

Based on your list from Question 4 above, add some of the detail given to produce a short but persuasive article of your own. You should write 150–200 words.

Example 5

Studies confirm roller-coaster and amusement park safety

The amusement industry is caught in a bizarre marketing and image dilemma. On the one hand, it wants to attract adrenaline junkies to ride the latest, greatest, biggest, meanest thrill rides at its theme parks and amusement parks. With names like 'Flight of Fear', 'Mind Eraser', and 'Lethal Weapon', parks brazenly position their marquee roller-coasters as extreme adventures that invoke terror and dread. On the other hand, the industry wants to reassure park-goers that despite the wild names – not to mention the mega-heights and speeds – thrill rides are actually quite safe and innocuous.

Bombarded by a rising tide of negative media reports, claims linking thrill rides to brain injuries, a congressional move to regulate amusement parks, and other attacks against the industry, Six Flags fired back last week by releasing the results of two scientific studies.

The bottom line: Theme parks and amusement parks in general, and roller-coasters in particular, are remarkably safe.

The American Association of Neurological Surgeons and Exponent Failure Analysis Associates, a scientific engineering research firm, conducted the independent studies, which Six Flags commissioned. A panel of experts, including doctors, engineers, NASA astronauts, and industry reps helped present and interpret the studies' findings at a Washington, D.C. press conference. Among the studies' highlights:

Amusement parks and theme parks are safer than other leisure activities

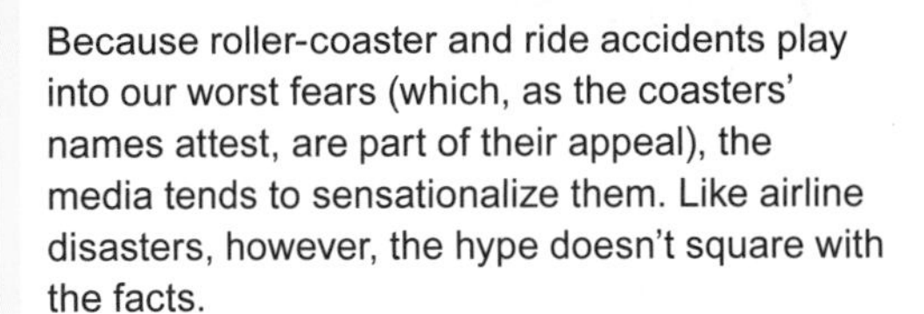

Because roller-coaster and ride accidents play into our worst fears (which, as the coasters' names attest, are part of their appeal), the media tends to sensationalize them. Like airline disasters, however, the hype doesn't square with the facts.

It is estimated that 319 million people visited parks in 2001. According to the association, the U.S. Consumer Product Safety Commission estimates that 134 park guests required hospitalization in 2001 and that fatalities related to amusement rides average two per year.

Extrapolating these numbers, riders have a 1 in 24 million chance of serious injury and a more than 1 in one-and-a-half billion chance of being fatally injured.

According to the studies, the injury rate for children's wagons, golf, and folding lawn chairs are higher than amusement rides.

The report also says that injury risk rates at amusement parks held steady from 1997 to 2001 and decreased over the last two years.

There is no research linking roller-coasters and brain injuries

Compared to the sustained forces astronauts or fighter pilots experience, the g-forces coasters exert are brief. While coaster heights and speeds have been rising, rates of acceleration and g-forces have remained relatively constant and within tolerable levels.

According to the studies, being hit with a pillow or falling on an exercise mat can cause much higher g-forces than a roller-coaster.

Arthur Levine
(http://themeparks.about.com)

Example 6

Fear is the key on the mother of all thrill rides

Does the new horror attraction at Orlando's Universal Studios live up to the hype? Beverley Fearis thinks it's a scream.

On Universal Studios' new star attraction, the least you can do is keep your eyes open. Blink and you'll miss out on millions of dollars' worth of special effects – and, with queues for this ride expected to reach up to an hour in peak season, you're not going to have time for a second chance.

Universal Studios

Billed as a fusion of threshold technology, high-speed roller-coaster engineering and space-age robotics, Revenge of the Mummy, according to its makers, heralds a new era in thrill rides. With 10 years of research and development behind it, the attraction carries riders at speeds of up to 45 miles per hour. It creates a smoke screen using 2,500 gallons of liquid nitrogen a day; blasts out 18,000 watts of sound through 200 speakers; conjures up flame effects with temperatures above 1,870°C; and features authentic-looking gleaming treasure made from more than 3,000 sheets of gold foil.

Breathtaking statistics aside, the key to the success of this four-minute ride is that it taps into all your physical and psychological fears – the dark, bugs, smoke, passing through doors into the unknown, falling, sudden movements, things that make you jump – in short, all the simple surprise and suspense elements of an old-fashioned ghost train. But forget the fluorescent-painted papier-mâché skeletons at the fairground, this is horror with a big, big, Hollywood budget.

'It takes the horror genre and stretches it as far as possible,' explains Stephen Sommers, director of the Mummy films and a collaborator on the attraction. 'The concept is to play against people's primal fears by fusing motion with very sophisticated special effects.'

The Mummy might not be the best film ever made (*The Mummy* Returns is slightly better) but it lends itself perfectly to a thrill ride, with skeletons, tombs, curses, lost souls, and, of course, mummies. One of the highlights of the ride is a 6ft 8in robotic figure of a mummy that Universal claims is the most realistic and fluid animated figure ever created. But the loudest screams come when riders plunge through a smoke screen into darkness (handy tip: this is when the dreaded photograph is taken) and when the car suddenly jerks backwards. Alongside all its other firsts, this is the first roller-coaster to employ both forward and backward motion.

Unlike older rides, where the roar of the vehicle against the tracks drowns out your screams, the tracks on this one are filled with sand to minimise noise. If, like me, your language rapidly deteriorates when under extreme pressure, remember there are children around. My advice is: keep your eyes open and your mouth shut.

As its newest ride, Revenge of the Mummy is set to be the park's biggest draw, but it's just one of many exhilarating attractions at Universal's two parks – Universal Studios and the Islands of Adventure next door.

From the *Observer*, 23 May 2004

Extension task

Examples 5 and 6 are pieces of stimulus material relating to theme parks. Example 5 is a newsletter from Six Flags, an American theme park, reporting on a scientific survey about safety issues and Example 6 is a newspaper report in which the journalist describes a ride on a roller coaster.

1. Write a magazine article in which you analyse why people find theme parks and their rides so popular. In particular, explain why they are not as dangerous as they might appear to be. You should refer closely to the stimulus material.
2. Your school has arranged a trip to a theme park. Write a letter to parents who may be worried by this, explaining why they should not be worried and what they are likely to enjoy about the trip. You should refer closely to the stimulus material.

Following on from this initial letter, further tasks could include another letter explaining the arrangements made for the trip (details of transport to the theme park, arrangements for supervision of the students during the trip, schedule for the day, etc.). As a conclusion to this unit of work students could produce a piece of imaginative writing describing their day out at the theme park.

(Teachers may use all or some of these materials in any way they wish to allow students to practise reading and writing skills.

- These examples could be also used as a basis for summary practice.
- Example 6, in particular, offers students the opportunity to write about the way the journalist uses language to convey his experiences on roller coasters.
- As well as using the passages independently it is also possible to combine them to produce a longer piece of work which students can do individually or by combining into small groups.)

Writing about media texts

When writing about media texts there are some other factors that it is important to pay attention to. The main points to consider are:

- **Audience**. It is important that you have a clear appreciation of the target audience at which the particular text is aimed. For example, different newspapers have different readerships and an awareness of this will help you to understand the intentions of a writer. For example, nearly all newspapers take a stated political stance. So, because the editor knows

that the paper sells mainly to people with particular political beliefs, or to people from particular socio-economic groups, then it is likely that the content of the articles will be angled to be sympathetic to those groups. Advertisements for the same item are worded differently when they appear in a glossy upmarket magazine from when they appear in a local newspaper.
- **Persuasion**. Media texts, in general, contain a particular bias for or against a specific belief, opinion, product, person, etc. The writers of these texts use all the skills they have to persuade you, the reader, to share their opinions. They are likely, therefore, to make use of emotive vocabulary and to present opinions as facts. In order to assess fairly what they are saying it is important to keep these underlying prejudices in mind – even if you are disposed to agree with the opinions expressed anyway!
- **Presentational features**. As mentioned earlier, writers of media texts will use devices other than just words to attract the interest of their readers. They will use headlines, subheadings, different typefaces and font sizes, straplines, columns and illustrations such as photographs, cartoon drawings and other diagrams to attract the readers' attention and to make their ideas attractive to their readers. When you write about media texts it is important to show that you are aware of these features and to attempt to explain why they are used and how effective they are.

Writing media texts

Writing media texts of the sort we have looked at earlier in this chapter is a somewhat specialised activity and is unlikely to be something that you will be asked to do in the examination.

Sometimes a Directed Writing task may be set in the format of a leaflet or a magazine article. In that case, do not be tempted to waste a lot of time on the layout or possible pictures. Remember as always that you are being assessed on your ability to write Standard English, not on your ability to lay out a page attractively.

In some circumstances, you may find it helpful to use a few of the techniques used by writers of these texts to achieve their effects, for example subheadings for paragraphs, picture captions, or a single-sentence paragraph to emphasise your overall message. But make sure that they are balanced by longer, connected paragraphs that demonstrate your writing skills.

However, another feature of media texts (especially of newspapers and magazines) is the writing of reports and reviews and we shall be looking at ways of approaching this in the following section. The first example is of a newspaper **report**.

Example 7

These articles are from two different news media giving reports of a cricket match between Sri Lanka and Pakistan and contain many features typical of report writing. Both of them give the details of the key features of the game and of the performances of the different players. The first report is from a Pakistani publication and the second from a Sri Lankan one.

Report 1

2nd T20: Pakistan pull off unbelievable win to take series

COLOMBO: Shahid Afridi and Anwar Ali played key roles as Pakistan ended a successful tour of Sri Lanka with a thrilling one-wicket victory in the second Twenty20 international in Colombo on Saturday.

Pakistan recovered from 40–5 in the eighth over to surpass Sri Lanka's challenging 172–7 with four balls to spare with Imad Wasim striking the winning six off left-arm seamer Binura Fernando.

Skipper Afridi led the way with a 22-ball 45 that included four sixes and a boundary, before Anwar smashed 46 off 17 balls in a match-winning knock that contained four sixes and three fours.

Imad, who remained unbeaten on 24, helped Anwar add 58 for the eighth wicket as the tourists recorded a heart-stopping win in front of a sell-out crowd of 35,000 at the Premadasa stadium that briefly included Sri Lanka President Maithripala Sirisena.

Pakistan v Sri Lanka 2nd T20 – as it happened

Pakistan, who won the first T20 match by 29 runs on Thursday, completed a remarkable treble on the six-week tour, having earlier won the Test series 2–1 and the one-dayers 3–2.

Fernando, a lean 20-year-old playing only his second international match, gave Sri Lanka a flying start with a double strike in his second over.

He bowled Ahmed Shehzad with a slower delivery and then forced Mukhtar Ahmed to top-edge a bouncer to Chamara Kapugedera at mid-wicket.

Pakistan's top order caved in as Mohammad Hafeez and Umar Akmal were run out and senior batsman Shoaib Malik was stumped.

Afridi began the amazing turnaround with a sixth-wicket stand of 61 with Mohammad Rizwan (17) as the inexperienced Sri Lankan attack wilted under pressure.

In the hosts' innings earlier, aggressive batting by debutant Shehan Jayasuriya and the recalled Kapugedera lifted Sri Lanka to 172–7 after skipper Lasith Malinga won the toss and elected to bat in the day-night match.

Jayasuriya, a 23-year-old left-hander unrelated to Sri Lanka's former captain Sanath Jayasuriya, smashed three fours and two sixes in his 32-ball 40 before he was fifth out.

But it was Kapugedera who boosted the total with an unbeaten 48 off 25 balls that contained four sixes and two boundaries.

Kapugedera put on 55 for the sixth wicket with Milinda Siriwardana (23) as the hosts plundered 59 runs in the final five overs. But it was not enough.

Report 2

Afridi, Ali whack Sri Lanka – beat SL by 1 wicket and seal series 2–0

By Anjana Kaluarachchi

CT Sports: Firm striking by Shahid Afridi (45) and Anwar Ali (46) turned the game around as Pakistan beat Sri Lanka by 1 wicket in a thrilling T20 played at R.Premadasa Stadium yesterday. Pakistan sealed the series 2–0.

Chasing 173 to win Pakistan were 40 for 5 in the 8th over, before Afridi started turning the tables as the visitors chased down the target in 19.2 overs, finishing with a six by Imad Wasim. Lasith Malinga again conceded the most number of runs, 40 in his 4 overs of the match.

Afridi smashed a 22 ball 45 which included 4 sixes, as he guided Pakistan past 100 in 13.2 overs with a partnership of 61 runs for the 6th wicket with Mohammad Rizwan (17).

Anwar Ali continued from there on with 46 from just 17 balls which included 4 sixes and 3 fours as he added 58 for the 8th wicket with Imad Wasim taking Pakistan to get 8 in 8 balls to win.

Binura Fernando playing his 2nd T20 was given 6 runs to defend in the last over, but Wasim took only one ball to finish things off after Mohammad Irfan took a single off the first ball.

The visitors lost both their openers in the 3rd over as Binura Fernando took the middle stump off Ahmed Shehzad, while Mukthar Ahmed gave an easy catch to Kapugedara at deep midwicket. Sri Lanka got two run outs, while Milinda Siriwardena foxed Shoaib Malik for an easy stumping, when the home team was in the driving seat.

Earlier in the match, in the home side's innings, comeback man Chamara Kapugedera proved a point again with a breathtaking 25 ball 48 runs, while debutant Shehan Jayasuriya made 40 at a crucial stage as Sri Lanka made 172 for 7 in their quota of 20 overs.

Kapugedera who remained unbeaten in both the T20 games, had 4 sixes and 2 boundaries in his innings as he added 55 in 34 deliveries for the seventh wicket with Milinda Siriwardana (23), and another 27 in 11 balls for the seventh wicket, which elevated the home team total to 172 after being 65–4 at the half way mark.

Sri Lanka made 50 in 6.2 overs but slumped in the run rate due to a slow innings by Dhananjaya de Silva, while Thisara Perera who was promoted to number 5, scored just 1 run as Sri Lanka added only 15 runs in the next 22 deliveries.

Debutant Jayasuriya smashed four and six in the 11th over from Pakistan skipper Shahid Afridi, taking back the momentum in his 32 ball 40 which included 3 fours and 2 sixes, before the Siriwardana and Kapugedera show started.

Thilakaratne Dilshan was lucky early on as he was dropped by Mohammad Hafeez at short midwicket, but Dilshan returned the favour just one ball apart as he hit straight to him again in the same over.

Sri Lanka made two changes in the team as Shehan Jayasuriya and Dasun Shanka made their debuts for the injured Angelo Mathews and Kithuruwan Vithanage.

Ceylon Today, 2 August 2015

Exercise 4

1 Choose one player in the match and compare what the two reports say about him. What are the differences in the details of events that they include and also in the tone of the writers and the language they use? When writing your comparison you should keep in mind the audience for which each report was intended. Then do the same for a section of the match, for example the start or the end.

2 Re-read both reports carefully and then write your own account of the match. Remember that in this sort of Directed Writing task, the Reading marks are based on the use you make of the information given in the text. So your report should be accurate and include all the important details. In this case it should also be focused on giving a factual and unbiased account of events to the reader.

Now we will look at an example of a **review** of the final film in Peter Jackson's 'Hobbit' trilogy.

Example 8

The Hobbit: The Battle of the Five Armies review – no more than a middling finale from Middle-earth

Despite the admirable Martin Freeman, this last film of a bloated trilogy offers few departures from a tried and tested formula

Mark Kermode, Observer film critic

Sunday 14 December 2014 09.30 GMT Last modified on Wednesday 7 January 2015 13.48 GMT

And so, in the end, we find ourselves once again at the beginning, having travelled there and back again in the company of elves, dwarves, dragons and hobbits – a journey which started 13 years (and more than 17 screen-hours) ago with the unveiling of *Lord of the Rings: The Fellowship of the Ring* in December 2001. Back then, the scope and scale of Peter Jackson's visual imagination was breathtaking. Animators like Ralph Bakshi had taken a crack at Tolkien's weighty tomes before, but Jackson was making game-changing use of computer graphics to blur the line between the 'real' and the 'imagined'. Having never cared for the source novels, I found myself wholly transported to Middle-earth, swept away by the sheer cinematic force of Jackson's vision. How long ago that all seems now.

Like the *Star Wars* prequels, the *Hobbit* movies were always destined to disappoint. Originally slated for direction as a two-parter by *Pan's Labyrinth* maestro Guillermo del Toro, the series returned to Jackson's helmsmanship following lengthy production delays, and promptly expanded into a trilogy via the addition of extraneous appendices and gender-balancing new characters (viz Evangeline Lilly's Tauriel). Yet like the haunted Thorin Oakenshield (a Shakespearean Richard Armitage), who spends much of this final movie holed up beneath the Lonely Mountain, bedazzled by an undulating sea of gold, one wonders whether the purity of Jackson's original quest hasn't been lost amid the series' shiny success. Fans of the first two *Hobbit* movies may not be disappointed by this final instalment, which offers few departures from the formula of yore, but those who remember the risks Jackson took with *Bad Taste*, *Braindead*, *Heavenly Creatures* and even his *King Kong* reboot may find themselves wishing for more than just more of the same.

We open with a spectacular pre-credits set piece in which the enraged dragon Smaug – once again voiced by a lizard-tongued Benedict Cumberbatch – lays siege to Lake-town, raining fire from the heavens. It's a bravura curtain-raiser, an air-raid orchestrated with a dynamic skill which suggests that Jackson's long-nurtured *Dam Busters* remake won't be short on blitzy spectacle. As buildings burn and innocents falter, Lake-town's greasy Master (Stephen Fry) attempts to make off with the loot, introducing a note of humour to the carnage ('if only we could save more people, but they're just not worth it'), selling his soul down the river as Bard the Bowman (Luke Evans) strikes out with his righteous arrows.

Sadly, little that follows can hold a candle to that kinetic opener. While the second *Hobbit* film, *The Desolation of Smaug*, largely dispensed with the endless tea-party pootlings of opener *An Unexpected Journey* to serve up a succession of fairground thrill-rides, *Five Armies* has more than its fair share of elaborately tressed actors reciting lumpen expository or emotional dialogue while brooding CGI landscapes roll endlessly in the background. It doesn't help that Jackson shoots every meeting with a panoramic swirl which accentuates the virtual artifice; although once hailed as a potential successor to David Lean, Jackson's cinematic instincts are here singly overshadowed by a computer game aesthetic. Even the more action-packed moments suffer from a superfluity of weightless runny-jumpy-stabby action better suited to *Assassin's Creed*, although a scene in which one of our many heroes leaps unfeasibly atop tumbling rocks makes him look less like Ezio than Super Mario; I half expected him to gather spinning gold coins en route. As for the titular final conflict, despite an abundance of goblins, trolls, bats, eagles and massive *Dune*/*Tremors*-style worms, it's no Battle of Helm's Deep. Yes, there's a lovely Kurosawa moment when the elves leap in formation over the shielded ranks of dwarves, catching their attackers unaware. But elsewhere, despite the much vaunted 'darkness' of this finale, it's a succession of clanging and banging that continues for what seems like an eternity – only without the sense of history in the making.

There are, of course, plus points, most notably the irrepressible Martin Freeman, who has made the role of Bilbo Baggins his own. With his flustered perseverance and tirelessly quizzical expression, Bilbo wrestles the prototypical Tolkien themes at the heart of this tale (the malady of riches, the corruption of power) with deceptive levity and engaging sprightliness. No wonder McKellen's perpetually pipe-smoking Gandalf is so keen on the little fellow; you really miss him when he's off screen, which is often, as the narrative slips hither and yon, variously addressing its multi-stranded distractions.

And what of the future? Since Jackson first set foot in Middle-earth we have seen the dawn of 'performance capture', which organically combines acting with computer graphics, and the widespread rejection of the faster 48 frames-per-second format in which studios and audiences alike seem to have lost both faith and interest. He leaves the Shire in rude health, the future of fantasy cinema changed forever by his work, the legacy of Tolkien solemnly enshrined in the annals of movie history.

Now it really is time to move on.

The purpose of a review is to give an account of the key features of, for example, a film or a concert and then for the writer of the review to give his or her opinion of the subject, commenting on its good and less good points with the intention either of helping the readers to decide whether they want to see the performance for themselves or, if it was a one-off performance, to let them know what it was like and what they would have experienced if they had been there themselves.

Regular readers of a newspaper will be familiar with the interests and tastes of the particular journalists who produce its reviews and this knowledge will also help the readers to make up their minds about the subject of the review.

In this example, the writer is reviewing the final film in a trilogy and is concerned with informing his readers about how well the final film in the series compares with those that came before. You may feel that in some places he seems to be more concerned with establishing his own past experience as a reviewer and as a man of good taste, or at least the same taste as his readers.

However, the review effectively summarises the plot (without giving too much away – the readers who are going to see the film don't want to know everything that happens); it comments authoritatively on the performances of the main actors and highlights what may be the less successful features of the film. It concludes with generally positive comments about the trilogy as a whole but questions the direction fantasy films will take in the future.

Exercise 5

Read carefully the review of *The Hobbit: The Battle of the Five Armies* and then:

1. Write brief, one-line notes of what the reviewer thought were the good *and* bad points of the film. It is not necessary to use your own words.
2. Now use your notes from Question 1 to write a summary of what the reviewer thought were the good *and* bad points of the film.

   Use your own words as far as possible. You will be awarded marks for producing a piece of writing which is relevant, well organised and easy to follow.

   Your summary must be in continuous writing (not note form). You are advised to write between 150 and 180 words, including the ten words given below.

   The reviewer had mixed feelings about the film's overall quality ...

Tips for writing reports and reviews

Here is a summary of the main points to remember when writing reviews or reports of this kind.

- **Be concise:** It is important that you convey key information relating to the subject of your writing as clearly and concisely as possible. Your readers will want to gain a swift overview of the main points and may not have time (or inclination) to wade through lengthy paragraphs of introductory comments.

- **Introduction:** Your introduction is particularly important as this is where you will engage your reader. It is important that you make clear the direction that your review will take, but, at the same time, the introduction should be sufficiently open-ended to encourage the reader to stay interested.
- **Give a balanced view:** You may have strong opinions about the subject of your writing and you should certainly express them, as long as they are justified by reference to events or examples. However, not everyone thinks the same as you do so it is important that you try to present a balanced assessment of your subject matter. Even if you are writing about something about which you have a very poor opinion, there are likely to be some more positive qualities that should be mentioned.
- **Remember your audience:** You may be writing a report of a sports fixture that involves a team you support. If you know that your readers are likely to share your support then you can legitimately spend much of the report writing about what 'your' team did; however, you must remember that the fixture involved another team as well and that that team's supporters will also want to know how their team played and yours might be the only report they see. Similarly, you may be a reviewing a book or film that you thought was too childish for your taste – but don't forget younger readers of your review may well enjoy the book or film, so try to include comments that will appeal to their point of view.
- **Conclusion:** Your conclusion should be as concise as your introduction: sum up the main points of your report or review; remind the reader what was good and less good about your subject and leave them with a general comment that will allow them to draw their own conclusions (guided by your comments, of course).

Punctuation: apostrophes

Apostrophes are used for two main purposes: to indicate when a letter or letters have been left out of a word; and to show possession. The first of these uses is quite easy to understand; the second can be more problematic.

- **Omission:** One way of giving your writing a more informal or colloquial tone is by *contracting* the form of some words. For example, in speech, most people would not say something like, 'I *do not* think that *we will* be able to go to the beach tomorrow. It *is not* a good day as there *will not* be any transport available.' Instead, they would use contracted forms of the words in italics. When you write such contracted forms, you must use apostrophes to show where letters have been left out; for example, 'I *don't* think that *we'll* be able to go to the beach tomorrow. It *isn't* a good day as there *won't* be any transport available.'
- **Possession:** In order to show possession (that is, to show the owner of something), an apostrophe, followed by the letter **–s** is put at the end of the noun indicating the person or thing that is the possessor when there is only one person or thing concerned. For example:

Possessor	Possessive form
Girl	The girl's dress
Boy	The boy's book
School	The school's classrooms

- However, if there is more than one possessor (where the plural form of the noun is indicated by the letter –**s**) then the possessive is shown by adding an apostrophe after the –**s** of the plural. For example:

Possessor	Possessive form
Girls	The girls' dresses
Boys	The boys' books
Schools	The schools' classrooms

Notes

1 When the plural of a noun is formed in a different way, *not* by adding –**s**, then the possessive is shown by –**'s**. For example: 'The men's changing room'; 'The women's changing room'; 'The children's playground'.
2 The only word that determines the position of the apostrophe is the noun indicating the possessor. Whether one person possesses many things or many people share the ownership of one thing, there is no deviation from the apostrophe rule. For example: 'The girl's presents' (one girl owning many presents) and 'The teachers' staffroom' (many teachers, but only one room).
3 The apostrophe should be used in expressions such as 'a week's holiday', 'a day's sickness', 'an hour's delay'.
4 The apostrophe is only used in the word *it's* when it is a contraction for *it is*. For example, 'It's a hot day today'. The apostrophe is *not* used in the possessive adjective *its*; for example, 'The dog ate its bone.' (Getting this wrong is a very common error; make a point of getting it right.)
5 There are two more common errors with apostrophes with the letter –**s** that you must never make in your writing: never use one in a verb form such as 'makes' or 'does'; and never use one in a plural when there is nothing being possessed or owned, such as *We sell tomatoes* or *Cats make good pets*.

Punctuation exercise

Rewrite the following sentences using apostrophes as required.

1 Jennys books were left in the schools dining room.
2 'Whats the matter with the cat? It cant seem to find its food.'
3 'Ive had at least a months wait for this letter; its about time something turned up.'
4 Mr Jones car was missing a hub cap.
5 The boys football had been lost among the gardens long grass.
6 'Whats this ball doing here? This is the Mayors private property.'
7 The birds nests were blown out of the trees by the winds force.
8 'Where are you going? Im not going with you; its too late.'

9 Both of the History teachers cars radiators were not working properly.
10 Mrs Smiths sons house wasnt very close to his wifes place of work.

Writing exercises on media texts

1 Write two reports of a sporting fixture that you attended. One report should be written for a national newspaper and the other for the club magazine of one of the sides taking part in the match.
2 Write a magazine review of a concert you attended, a film or television programme you watched or a music CD. You should attempt to be balanced in your comments.
3 A friend and his or her family are planning to take a holiday to a place that you know well. Write a report on the place for them in which you comment on its good and bad features and say which of the features will appeal to the different members of the family.
4 As a successful student in your school you have been asked to write an article for your local newspaper in which you review what you have learnt during your time at the school and explain what it has to offer other students. Write your report.

Extension task

(This can be done as a small group activity with each member of the group producing a different section.)

Think about an issue of local, national or international importance about which you have strong feelings. Produce your own media campaign (pamphlets, letters, website material, etc.) through which you hope to encourage others to share your concerns.

7 FICTION: PROSE NARRATIVES

Reading prose narratives

Prose narratives are novels and short stories, and are texts that tell a story. Unlike personal writing, they are usually imaginary. Most of the examples of writing that we have seen in earlier chapters have been relatively short, or broken up into sections, similar to the length of the passages you will be tackling in the examination. However, in this chapter we will be concentrating on how writers put together longer works. Almost always the narrative passage you are asked to read and answer questions on in the examination is taken from a longer work, and a typical question can explore themes like how the writer shapes a description to lead on into the story, or how he or she builds up the tension before the next piece of action. The exercises on the passages in this chapter aim to show you how the answers to those individual questions can fit together to make a more general critical review of the whole piece, and to give you practice in doing it. When it comes to the examination, having an idea of what the questions are aiming to explore will help you to distinguish what sort of information each question is asking for: the facts from the passage or the reason for including them, what the imagery is or its effect.

Obviously within the time constraints of an examination you will not be asked to write a complete novel or even a full short story. Consideration of the techniques used by the writers of the stories contained in this chapter should help you, however, to gain the skills required to write your own story in the examination if you choose one of the narrative topics. But there are also occasions when it is useful to think about what you are writing as part of a longer work, the introduction perhaps to introduce the characters, or a description of the setting which ends with the door opening ... It gives a convincing focus to your choice of details and vocabulary. And it often gives you a suitable point for a cliff-hanger ending.

Writing prose narratives involves two key skills; one is to relate the events in the story itself, making sure that the reader has a clear awareness of the sequence of events. The second is more complex and involves producing a narrative that is an entertaining and effective piece of writing. In order to judge whether a writer has done this successfully it is necessary to consider certain key elements that have to be convincing as well as the story itself. These include:

- **Setting.** The setting of a story simply means the place or places in which the events of the story happen. No matter what the subject matter of the story is, it is important that its setting is convincing to the reader and that it is both consistent with and appropriate to the events being described. For example, a setting featuring a mysterious and scary old house with creaking doors and ceilings covered with spiders' webs is a likely background for a ghost story. However, such a story could also take place in a modern housing development where everything is apparently normal until unusual, mysterious events start happening. Both of these contrasting settings can produce perfectly effective ghost stories as long as they stay consistent. If the writer suddenly 'forgets' his overall setting and describes the next few actions as taking place in a creaking, haunted, old house instead of a modern house (or a modern house in the middle of a wild and ghostly landscape), the setting becomes less convincing and the reader becomes distracted into thinking about the discrepancies instead of remaining fully engaged in the story. A good writer will avoid mistakes such as these.

- **Characterisation.** Just as it is important for the setting of a story to be convincing, it is equally important that the characters who feature in the story are portrayed as believable human beings within its setting. For a story to be effective, it is important that the reader can identify with some or all of the characters and that those characters should be convincing and come across as real people. Again, it is important that they are seen to be natural inhabitants of the story's setting: a fantasy landscape and setting requires mainly larger than life, fantastic inhabitants. However, for a fantasy story to be fully convincing for its readers at least one of the central characters must have enough of the characteristics of an 'ordinary' human being so that the readers of the story – who are 'ordinary' human beings themselves, and not fantasy heroes – can have a point of reference in whom they can believe and with whom they can identify.
- **Structure.** Over 2000 years ago, the ancient Greek philosopher Aristotle made the point that a story should have a beginning, middle and an end. This observation still holds true today. A good story should be carefully planned and structured in order to keep the readers interested and to ensure that the sequence of events is clear and easily followed. The best stories are not written by writers who make up events as they go along, but are carefully planned and thought out before writing begins. When we talk about the 'structure' of a story, we are really considering the way in which this planned sequence of events develops. A successful story does not have to cover a range of exciting and heroic action leading to a devastating climax – it can be much more low-key than that and the resolution of the story can involve what is no more than an everyday action. For example, the story could be about the experience of a very shy boy who finally plucks up the courage to speak to the girl he passes every day on the way to school. As long as the writer has presented the situation leading up to this decision convincingly, the ending to the story will achieve greater significance than we would expect from a simple summary of what happens. It is also worth keeping in mind that although the beginning, middle and end of a story refer to the time scheme of events within the story, the structure imposed on these events by the writer does not have to present them in this order. For example, a detective story could start with the sentencing of a criminal and then tell the story of what led to his arrest in flashback.
- **Language.** It is through the language they use in their stories that writers make the most immediate communication with their readers. It is,

therefore, very important that they ensure that their choice of words, sentence structures, etc. is appropriate to the events being described and the characters who feature in them. Their descriptions of the setting must bring the places being described to life, and allow the readers to feel confident that they can visualise the places in which the events of the story take place. Similarly, the vocabulary used to describe the thoughts of a character should be able to convey that character's individual nature as convincingly as possible. With short stories in particular, writers must establish setting and character as convincingly as possible in a relatively succinct way – the very nature of short story writing means that writers are unable to indulge in the leisurely, lengthy descriptions and scene-setting that might be used in a novel where length is not a consideration.

The points above contain some of the key things to look for when you are reading a short story and considering what makes it good. It is now time to look at some examples and some exercises based on them. The following passages make up a complete short story written by a West Indian author; the first is from the opening; the next is from the middle of the story and the third is from the ending. The questions that follow the extracts will focus both on testing how well you have understood what you have read and also on your appreciation of the structure of the story and of the writer's use of language.

Passage 1

Seashells

I was going down Breadnut Hill on my way to Saturday market when I heard a big commotion and saw a crowd of people round a big hospital-looking van parked at the roundabout. Somebody flashed past me yelling, 'Whoi, whoi, people, run come here! See they putting Lena inna 'sylum van! They putting Lena inna 'sylum van!'

It was my best friend Clancy's mother's sister. Two twos, before I could draw breath, Clancy herself brushed past me like lightning. 'Come on, Annette!'

After her, a whole crowd of people started coming out of their yards, running towards the van. I ran after everybody else just in time to see two policemen hoist Lena into the van and slam the door shut.

Lena's face looked out at us through the window. It looked the way it always did, like a clown's mask, all white with powder, and three red slashes on her mouth and cheeks. But this time she looked angry. It was the first I saw Lena look anything but serene. She looked like a ruffled whitefaced hen. Even though I was puzzled and scared, it made me want to laugh.

'What they taking Lena away for?' I asked Mr Glenn, who was standing next to me. 'What she do?'

Mr Glenn, didn't answer. People were surrounding the van and shouting and refusing to move. The policemen waved batons but still the crowd didn't move, and more people were coming.

'What you taking her away for, Officer? What she do?'

'So, you recruiting madpeople now for the police force?'

'But Lena don't trouble nobody! Look how much years now she peaceful. How long she mad on the street and peaceful.'

But the policemen shoved some people aside and got in the van and drove off.

Miss Prescott's son Peril, whom everybody called City Puss, shouted, 'But this is thiefery, you know! Thiefing the woman from off the street like that.'

Some people laughed, because everybody knew City Puss was the biggest thief in town. That's why they called him City Puss, because he stole worse than a cat, but in big style. City Puss stole fit for a city, not a small market town.

A policeman stuck his head through the window and shouted back, 'So she belong to somebody? You want me to pay you money for her?'

Lena was sitting in the window looking at us with that comical, annoyed look on her face. When the van got to the corner she waved, slow and regal, like an African queen. It was like she thought she was in a movie and somebody should take her picture.

People started quarrelling and saying how the police was so rude, somebody should put a stop to them, and how they can come in the town and move out a madwoman without saying anything to anybody? There were some people who didn't belong to the town but had just come in to do their business. They said the same.

But the van was gone, so there was nothing anybody could do. Mr Glenn, who lived on the avenue by the police station, said he would go down there and investigate, but he couldn't do it now because he was fixing shoes in his shop. Everybody was busy because it was market morning, so people just grumbled a bit more and said, 'Awright Mr Glenn, you check it out and mek we know,' and went back to their business.

Nobody believed Lena was in any real danger. They were just mad at the police for bad manners and not satisfying their curiosity. Lena had been our madwoman for ages and ages. Everybody knew her, including the police. We knew it was nothing serious and they would bring her back.

I hurried up quick quick to buy the things Aunt Vera sent me to buy because I didn't want her getting mad for I was staying too long.

But the police didn't bring Lena back. In the evening we heard on the news they were rounding up streetpeople and taking them to safe places where they could be looked after. Apart from Lena, they had

→

rounded up lots of people in the parish and taken them in.

People in Lucea town were hopping mad.

Aunt Vera never paid Lena any mind, but now she said, 'Streetpeople, which streetpeople? You see Lena is any streetpeople? Look how long Lena live among us mad as shad and we taking care of her and she not troubling anybody nor causing no nuisance to government! Streetpeople what? Streetpeople where?'

Clancy and I didn't know what to think. Lena was like fixture in Lucea town and we couldn't imagine passing the leaking hydrant on our way to school or going by the beach and not seeing Lena. What the people said was true. Lena was mad longer than for ever, but it was a nice mad.

She was tall and stately with fair skin and lots and lots of hair which she coiled in a bun and pushed under a neat jippy-jappa hat with side ribbons. She was always dressed neat and squeaky clean in long straw-coloured skirts and matching blouses. She had all these rows of pale-coloured beads around her neck. She pasted white powder on her face so thick it looked like somebody had their face in a cast. On top of the powder on her cheeks and lips she plastered red red rouge and lipstick like blood.

Lena never troubled anybody. She just used to come out every morning with her straw basket on her arm, full of bathing things, and stop at the leaking fire hydrant in front of the post office and wash herself and put on her makeup again. That took her from dawn to about nine o'clock.

If you passed by her she said, 'You bathe since morning?'

If you were stupid enough to answer, 'Yes, Lena,' and stand, she would say, 'Is true? Mek me see in your nosehole,' and she would grab your face and peep down into your nose.

You had to say, 'Yes, Lena,' and run.

The hydrant wasn't the only place Lena washed herself. She liked to have another set of wash at midday, but by then the sun was real hot, so she went down to the sea. During school holidays Clancy and me saw her by the beach a whole lot, because we were always going there to look for shells and coloured rocks and kick our feet in the breakers and sometimes, when no adults were looking, swim out to the buoys.

Lena was almost always there. She used to stand at the edge and throw seawater on her face, dry off, then make up again. Then she would walk out into the water and come back up the beach gathering shells, like us. She had this habit of putting the shells to her ears and then putting them in front of her eyes and shaking them and hissing her teeth, then flinging them away. It was like she was listening for something in the shells that she never heard.

If she saw us gathering shells, she hissed her teeth and said, 'Lef the shell alone, idiot. You bathe since morning?' And Clancy and me'd laugh and I'd run.

Boldface Clancy didn't run, she just cocked her bottom at an angle and went sideways like a crab so if Lena tried to grab at her nose she could run. Lena noticed Clancy was set to run so she never troubled her. But one time Clancy with her boldface pushed up her hand and poked Lena's face to see if it would come off, and Lena lifted her basket and swatted Clancy one swat on her hand with it.

'Rude,' Lena muttered, sounding like Aunt Vera scolding. Clancy yowled and sucked her bruised knuckles. She never touched Lena again, but still she didn't run. Mostly Lena just ignored us, gathering shells and walking in the sea. When she'd satisfied herself, she'd climb up the beach back into town. By sunset she was back at the hydrant, washing her plaster-cast face again.

People in restaurants gave her food. Aunt Vera said nobody ran her out of the restaurants because Lena knew how to be a lady. She carried herself like a queen. She liked to clean the restaurant people's bathrooms in return for her food. The bathrooms didn't need any cleaning because the people had workers to clean them. But Lena cleaned them anyway.

One time Clancy and me went in the Kentucky Fried Chicken bathroom and Lena came in.

'You flush the toilet?' she said in her gruff voice that didn't fit her whitey-whitey appearance.

'Yes, Lena,' Clancy said, though we hadn't used the toilet at all. We went in to try out Clancy's new lipstick that she bought and hid because we were too young. Clancy just wanted to see what Lena would do.

'Let me see,' Lena said, and opened the toilet door. I got scared. The bathroom was a confined space. Suppose she decided to hold us down and look in our noses? Lena was tall and big and I was little and skinny and Clancy wasn't so big either. I turned tail and ran. Clancy ran after, but she was mad.

'You wouldn't even wait to see what she go do,' she accused me angrily. 'I wanted to see if she would wash her face in the toilet water. People say she wash her face anywhere she see water.'

'Yuck!' I said, disgusted more with Clancy than Lena. But I wondered how come the skin on Lena's face never peeled off with so much washing. Maybe it did. Maybe that's why she put the powder cast on.

Exercise 1

In previous chapters, the questions asked about the passages have mostly been about individual details of the content or the language, and sometimes you have been asked to go back and put those details together to create a longer response dealing with a longer part of the passage. The following questions are asking you to do the same exercise of sorting out the relevant details and then putting them together, but this time you have to identify the details yourself. There are some hints to help you tackle each of the questions.

1 From what you have read so far, what have you learnt about the appearance and character of Lena? Answer as fully as you can.

Start by making notes of all the details of Lena's appearance that the writer gives – there are quite a few, and they are straightforward. Her character, on the other hand, has to be deduced from what she says and does. Again there is quite a lot of information, but remember that the narrator who is telling you about Lena is writing from a child's viewpoint, which may modify your impressions. Then look at your two lists and think about how you will put all the information together to make a coherent whole. The passage says many times that Lena is a madwoman; that gives you a focus round which to construct your description. Are there details of her appearance that suggest she is mad, and others that suggest she is not? And the same for her actions. Think about how you will order your details, putting comments that apply to the same feature together perhaps and removing repetitions. Then write your description.

2 Consider how well the writer has created a convincing setting for this story.

Before you start noting the details for your answer, note that the question has asked you for a judgement: how convincing the setting is. This is your focus, and slightly less straightforward than Question 1. You have to think about what would make a convincing setting for this story, and then put together the details you find in the passage to make the picture and decide whether it matches. Has the writer told you enough? Or are there a lot of extra details that don't fit? Remember that it is not just the physical description that gives you the setting. Clues can also be given by things like how the people talk and what they are doing. Work through the same sequence as in Question 1, and be aware that even if it does not explicitly say so, this sort of question always requires you to make close reference to the text in your answer.

3 What makes this section an effective opening for the story? You should refer to the text in your answer.

If you have not already read to the end, you will probably feel you need to skim through the rest of the story before you answer this question, but the detail to consider is all in this section. Look back at what we said at the beginning of the chapter about setting, characterisation, structure and language. What decisions has the writer made about how to present the story? Is the setting consistent? Are the characters and the way they interact believable? What part of the story comes first? Is there anything that looks forward to the rest of the story and its ending? How do these features combine to make an effective opening? Although the question assumes that you will agree it is effective, you don't have to! But whether you agree or not you have to give your reasons and the evidence for them.

Passage 2

The day after they took Lena away hell broke loose in Lucea town and Mandeville. Mandeville people came out on the streets demonstrating because a whole tonload of streetpeople suddenly appeared on their clean clean streets where was no streetpeople before. Nobody could tell where they came from. Lucea people started to demonstrate because Lena's people came out in the town cussing and swearing to prosecute whoever took Lena, and they had better bring her back. So the townpeople went and joined them.

That was when Clancy and me knew that Lena had people. We always used to wonder where she came from. We figured she must live with somebody to have such nice clothes and look so neat, even though she washed at the fire hydrant. It turned out her people lived in Granville and every morning Lena got money to take the bus so she could do her daily work washing herself at the fire hydrant.

'I guess it keep her occupied,' Clancy said facetiously. 'People say having no work can drive you mad. They don't want her to get mad.'

'You idiot. Lena mad already.'

'Not really. She just quiet.'

'So because she's quiet, she can't be mad?'

'Huhn-huhn. But not Lena. You ever see mad person so neat?'

'Maybe she a neatness freak. Maybe that her kind of madness.'

'Or maybe she tired how the town damn dirty. After how many years she can't get nobody to follow her example. She will be glad she reach at clean cool Mandeville.'

'Mandeville can't suit Lena. It don't have neither sea nor river.'

'It have fire hydrant though. What the hell Lena doing with sea and river?'

I hissed my teeth because I could see Clancy just wanted an opportunity to swear 'damn' and 'hell', and now she got it. I ran off and left her and went to join the demonstration.

The demonstration was sweet because people dressed up and painted their faces like Jonkunnu and played loud music and waved funny placards. One lady had a placard that said, GIVE WE BACK. WE MADPEOPLE. EVERYTHING YOU ALL SEE POOR PEOPLE HAVE, YOU WANT IT. I got to dance to all the nice musics Aunt Vera would corn me if she caught me listening to. It was like Christmas.

But the demonstration spread and got nasty. This is how it went. Some people from the Citizens for Justice and the Society for the Prevention of Cruelty to Streetpeople came, and TV with big cameras. At first it was funny. The TV people asked a fat lady why she was demonstrating. The fat lady laughed and said, 'I don't really know, you know, sar. I passing and see the excitement so I join it too.' She skinned her gold tooth wide wide

for the camera. Later she must was happy because it came on TV.

The TV people asked the Citizens for Justice and they said a lot of things I didn't understand about injustice to streetpeople and streetpeople rights and how the streetpeople would suffer from when they were taking the Citizens for Justice lady's picture. She wanted to come on TV too. The police came and threw teargas and Clancy got some in her mouth and was sick for days. She didn't come on the TV.

In the end the government got in trouble because the TV people found out the police took out all those streetpeople to clean up Lucea town and took them to mess up cool clean Mandeville. They didn't take them to any safe place at all at all. The government had to promise to investigate. The police got in their vans and went and got back most of the streetpeople and put them on the street again.

But they didn't bring back Lena. Lena couldn't be found.

Clancy said, 'Let's go and ask the Citizens for Justice and the Prevention of Cruelty people to help find Lena.'

'Who, me? No way, Jose.'

I wasn't going anywhere with madhead Clancy. No way was I going to these people to show off so I could be told I was just a child and to leave bigpeople business alone. I was always having to rescue Clancy from all sorts of ambitious schemes. I never knew a girl so, always trying to act like she was big.

Furthermore, the Prevention and Citizens people were busy. After most of the streetpeople came back, a big advertisement from them appeared in the newspaper saying JUSTICE HAS BEEN SERVED. WE STAND FOR THE PEOPLE. The Citizens and Preventioners had a big rally commemorating the anniversary of the streetpeople's return. They put on a big streetplay showing how it had all happened, how the streetpeople were taken away and how they were fought for and returned. The head lady was a very good actress and it was really great fun to watch. I couldn't believe how they made the baglady and drughead costumes so realistic.

Exercise 2

1 How does this episode of the story help you to understand further the attitudes and behaviour of (a) the people from Mandeville, (b) the people of Lucea, (c) the police?

In this section Lena is not present, as she has been taken away, and the focus shifts to the wider population around her and their reactions to her and to what has happened. You will probably find it easiest to take one of the three groups at a time, and make notes of each time they are mentioned. It is always useful for this sort of question to ask 'Why?' So don't just write, 'The people from Mandeville came out on the streets demonstrating', but ask, 'Why did the people from Mandeville come out on the streets demonstrating?' That will lead you to think about what sort of people they were, their attitudes, as well as what they did, their behaviour. And then there's a second layer of 'Why?' Why did the writer include that detail? What impression does it make on the reader?

2 Explain as fully as you can how this section of the story develops from the previous section and provides the reader with a fuller understanding of events.

We have already seen in several contexts that the words 'explain how' in a question require more in your response than just the facts given in the passage. So start with the facts: what the police did, who told them to do it, how the different groups of people reacted, how the truth came out, etc. Then – since you are asked how they develop from the first section – look for the links. For example, people were upset and cross in the first section; did they stay upset and cross and what did they do as a result? And then consider the development. How does the writer introduce the new facts? For example, does the circle of people widen, and what is the result of their actions? Does the reader end up knowing everything he or she might want to know? There is, of course, one substantial loose end left, and that provides the link to the next passage.

Passage 3

Then one day, long long after all the excitement died down, I was sitting by the sea and Lena came.

I was sitting there feeling sad because I had to go away to boarding school, and Clancy was staying.

I was there wondering what I was going to do without my best friend.

'You bathe since morning?' a familiar voice said behind me.

I turned around faster than light.

She looked different. Her clothes were tattered like she hadn't changed them for a long time. You could see they had been washed over and over but they weren't very clean. She didn't have her jippy-jappa any more and her hair needed combing. It looked like she had tried, but hadn't done a good job of it. She also didn't have her straw basket with the cleaning things in. She had a conch shell. It was white with blue streaks the veins. I wondered where she got it from. There were no conch shells on this beach, so she must have got it from wherever she was coming from.

'Lena!' I cried, so relieved I forgot she was mad. 'Lena, where you come from? Where you was?'

Lena stood over me looking down. 'Face want wash,' she said disapprovingly.

It was true. I had been crying and then I wiped my hand in the sand and wiped it in my face. I could feel the sand grains like rough, sticky tears.

➜

I laughed. 'Is eyewater, Lena,' I said. 'It fossilize on m' face.'

Something seemed to connect because she jumped like somebody had come to arrest her again. 'Eyewater? Eyewater? What you have eyewater for? Anybody trouble you?'

I didn't know Lena had so many words in her head. Suddenly it didn't feel stupid to be talking to this madwoman. 'I going to boarding school and I go miss my friend,' I told her, like I was talking to somebody real. 'But where you come from, Lena? Where you was all this time?'

She was looking at me like she was hearing something else. 'Who trouble you? Somebody trouble you? Here, tek this.' She pushed out her arm in a sudden way, all jerky, and gave me the shell. I was so surprised I took it before I realized.

Lena gazed at me earnestly. 'Listen up,' she said. 'Hold it up and listen up. World in there.'

I put the shell to my ear and listened. I heard a sound like the sea was inside and it was so soft and whispery and wonderful and sad, I wanted to laugh and cry and fall asleep and run all at the same time. Lena watched me anxiously for a while. I closed my eyes to hear the shell better, but I could still feel her watching me.

Finally she squatted down beside me. 'World in there. Lena listen, Lena listen. Lena listen and follow the sound come back home.'

'You mean when you were there in Mandeville, where it don't have no sea, is the shell show you how to find back here 'cause it tell you to walk by the sea?'

Lena looked at me blankly as if I was mad. Then it looked like she lost focus, for she just got up and walked out into the water far away from me. I sat there watching her and listening sometimes to the waves in the sea and sometimes to the sea in the shell.

After a long time she came back up to the beach and she had a lot of little shells in her hand. I held out her big conch shell and said politely, 'Thank you, Lena, that was very nice.'

'Keep it. You don't want it?' Lena looked disgusted. Then she said, 'Lena reach home now. Keep it. Idiot.' Then she hissed her teeth and went up the beach into the town, leaving me holding the shell.

When I left I took Lena's shell with me. Nights when I felt really homesick I sat up in bed in the dorm and put it to my ear and listened to Lena's world of the sea. It made me feel better.

Nobody ever found out how Lena got home from Mandeville. But when I told Aunt Vera about the shell, she agreed with me that maybe Lena found or stole the shell somewhere and it somehow reminded her of where she came from, so she just walked along the coast roads until she got to where she recognized.

We will never know. But the journey and the shell seemed to change Lena in some way. I guess the way going to boarding school changed me. Aunt Vera said it was all part of growing up. I guess we both were growing up, Lena and me.

Clancy wrote and said Lena was OK again. Her people in Granville took her back in and she had new clean clothes and a new basket and fresh rouge and lipstick. Redder than ever, Clancy said. But she didn't wash by the fire hydrant any more. Now she washed only in the sea. Clancy said any time of day you went down by the beach you could see Lena, either washing herself or walking along the shoreline combing the beach for shells. It was like she felt she had lost the sea that time they took her to Mandeville, and she didn't want to risk losing it any more. Maybe she thought if she stayed by it all the time, she could keep it from going away, Clancy said.

I just hoped she found a shell with worlds inside, like the one she gave me. Because at boarding school whenever I was lonely, Lena's shell made me feel like I was safe and coming home.

From *Flying with Icarus and other stories* by Curdella Forbes

Exercise 3

1 What makes this final passage an effective conclusion to the story? Explain in detail the narrator's thoughts and feelings and what she has learnt from her meetings with Lena.

The final words of this question give you the main clue as to what this whole short story is really about, and what you should judge 'effective' against. But as always, start with the facts of what happens. How do they grow out of the two previous passages and how are they linked in? Do they leave the reader with a satisfied sense that the end of the story has been reached? Then consider the narrator's thoughts and feelings, which are more evident in this passage than they have been earlier. Why is that? What has she learnt? Finally think about why this is the third passage of quite a long short story. The story could just have started with 'One day Lena gave me a shell …'. Why did the writer decide to write all the detail of the streetpeople being taken away and other people's reactions to it?

2 Now that you have read the whole story, write a critical account of it. You should consider the development of the story and the ways in which the different episodes further your understanding. You should also consider the ways in which the author has presented the characters involved in the story and the language she uses.

If you put together all your work so far on this story, you have gone a long way towards answering this much more general question. But before you leave it, read it through and consider whether having all the material in one sequence suggests any other ideas to you. All good writing has many layers of meaning and response, and successful reading depends on being open to everything the writer is trying to convey.

Further reading exercises on narrative texts

Passage 4

Here is the opening of a short story by H.G. Wells.

The Door in the Wall

One confidential evening, not three months ago, Lionel Wallace told me this story of the Door in the Wall. And at the time I thought that so far as he was concerned it was a true story.

He told it me with such direct simplicity of conviction that I could not do otherwise than believe in him. But in the morning, in my own flat, I woke to a different atmosphere; and as I lay in bed and recalled the things he had told me, stripped of the glamour of his earnest slow voice, denuded of the focused, shaded table light, the shadowy atmosphere that wrapped about him and me, and the pleasant bright things, the dessert and glasses and napery of the dinner we had shared, making them for the time a bright little world quite cut off from everyday realities, I saw it all as frankly incredible. 'He was mystifying!' I said, and then: 'How well he did it! … It isn't quite the thing I should have expected of him of all people, to do well.'

Afterwards as I sat up in bed and sipped my morning tea, I found myself trying to account for the flavour of reality that perplexed me in his impossible reminiscences, by supposing they did in some way suggest, present, convey – I hardly know which word to use – experiences it was otherwise impossible to tell.

Well, I don't resort to that explanation now. I have got over my intervening doubts. I believe now, as I believed at the moment of telling, that Wallace did to the very best of his ability strip the truth of his secret for me. But whether he himself saw, or only thought he saw, whether he himself was the possessor of an inestimable privilege or the victim of a fantastic dream, I cannot pretend to guess. Even the facts of his death, which ended my doubts for ever, throw no light on that.

That much the reader must judge for himself.

I forget now what chance comment or criticism of mine moved so reticent a man to confide in me. He was, I think, defending himself against an imputation of slackness and unreliability I had made in relation to a great public movement, in which he had disappointed me. But he plunged suddenly. 'I have,' he said, 'a preoccupation –'

'I know,' he went on, after a pause, 'I have been negligent. The fact is – it isn't a case of ghosts or apparitions – but – it's an odd thing to tell of, Redmond – I am haunted. I am haunted by something – that rather takes the light out of things, that fills me with longings …'

He paused, checked by that English shyness that so often overcomes us when we speak of moving or grave or beautiful things. 'You were at Saint Athelstan's all through,' he said, and for a moment that seemed to me quite irrelevant. 'Well' – and he paused. Then very haltingly at first, but afterwards more easily, he began to tell of the thing that was hidden in his life, the haunting memory of a beauty and happiness that filled his heart with insatiable longings, that made all the interests and spectacle of worldly life seem dull and tedious and vain to him.

Now that I have the clue to it, the thing seems written visibly in his face. I have a photograph in which that look of detachment has been caught and intensified. It reminds me of what a woman once said of him – a woman who had loved him greatly. 'Suddenly,' she said, 'the interest goes out of him. He forgets you. He doesn't care a rap for you – under his very nose …'

Yet the interest was not always out of him, and when he was holding his attention to a thing Wallace could contrive to be an extremely successful man. His career, indeed, is set with successes. He left me behind him long ago; he soared up over my head, and cut a figure in the world that I couldn't cut – anyhow. He was still a year short of forty, and they say now that he would have been in office and very probably in the new Cabinet if he had lived. At school he always beat me without effort – as it were by nature. We were at school together at Saint Athelstan's College in West Kensington for almost all our school time. He came into the school as my co-equal, but he left far above me, in a blaze of scholarships and brilliant performance. Yet I think I made a fair average running. And it was at school I heard first of the 'Door in the Wall' – that I was to hear of a second time only a month before his death.

To him at least the Door in the Wall was a real door, leading through a real wall to immortal realities. Of that I am now quite assured.

And it came into his life quite early, when he was a little fellow between five and six. I remember how, as he sat making his confession to me with a slow gravity, he reasoned and reckoned the date of it. 'There was,' he said, 'a crimson Virginia creeper in it – all one bright uniform crimson, in a clear amber sunshine against a white wall. That came into the impression somehow, though I don't clearly remember how, and there were horse-chestnut leaves upon the clean pavement outside the green door. They were blotched yellow and green, you know, not brown nor dirty, so that they must have been new fallen. I take it that means October. I look out for horse-chestnut leaves every year and I ought to know.

'If I'm right in that, I was about five years and four months old.'

He was, he said, rather a precocious little boy – he learned to talk at an abnormally early age, and he was so sane and 'old-fashioned', as people say, that he was

➜

permitted an amount of initiative that most children scarcely attain by seven or eight. His mother died when he was two, and he was under the less vigilant and authoritative care of a nursery governess. His father was a stern, pre-occupied lawyer, who gave him little attention and expected great things of him. For all his brightness he found life grey and dull, I think. And one day he wandered.

He could not recall the particular neglect that enabled him to get away, nor the course he took among the West Kensington roads. All that had faded among the incurable blurs of memory. But the white wall and the green door stood out quite distinctly.

As his memory of that childish experience ran, he did at the very first sight of that door experience a peculiar emotion, and attraction, a desire to get to the door and open it and walk in. And at the same time he had the clearest conviction that either it was unwise or it was wrong of him – he could not tell which – to yield to this attraction. He insisted upon it as a curious thing that he knew from the very beginning – unless memory has played him the queerest trick – that the door was unfastened, and that he could go in as he chose.

I seem to see the figure of that little boy, drawn and repelled. And it was very clear in his mind, too, though why it should be so was never explained, that his father would be very angry if he went in through that door.

Wallace described all these moments of hesitation to me with the utmost particularity. He went right past the door, and then, with his hands in his pockets and making an infantile attempt to whistle, strolled right along beyond the end of the wall. There he recalls a number of mean dirty shops, and particularly that of a plumber and decorator with a dusty disorder of earthenware pipes, sheet lead, ball taps, pattern books of wallpaper, and tins of enamel. He stood pretending to examine these things, and coveting, passionately desiring, the green door.

Then, he said, he had a gust of emotion. He made a run for it, lest hesitation should grip him again; he went plumb with outstretched hand through the green door and let it slam behind him. And so, in a trice, he came into the garden that has haunted all his life.

It was very difficult for Wallace to give me his full sense of that garden into which he came.

There was something in the very air of it that exhilarated, that gave one a sense of lightness and good happening and well-being; there was something in the sight of it that made all its colour clean and perfect and subtly luminous. In the instant of coming into it one was exquisitely glad – as only in rare moments, and when one is young and joyful one can be glad in this world. And everything was beautiful there …

Exercise 4

1 By referring closely to this extract, write out as fully as you can what you have learnt about:
- Lionel Wallace
- the narrator
- the story that Wallace told.

You should use your own words, but remember to quote from the passage.

The question is asking for facts, what the passage says, but remember that some things you learn by deduction, rather than being told directly. For instance, it is clear almost from the start that this is not a modern story. How do you know? Is it the language used? Or some of the details of the description? And what occupation did the two men have?

2 Consider fully why this is an effective opening to the story. In particular, you should think about:
- the writer's narrative standpoint
- the setting of the story
- any clues that are given as to how the story might develop and which will make readers want to know what will happen next
- the language used by the writer.

The narrator doesn't tell the story about himself; he looks back and recounts how it was told to him (a story within a story). Why do you think he does this? What does it enable him to do? What effect does it have on the story? On the setting?

3 For each of the words underlined in the passage, write down the letter which has the same meaning as the word has in the passage.

a conviction

A confidence **B** feeling **C** faith **D** principle

b perplexed

A surprised **B** puzzled **C** worried **D** upset

c reticent

A reserved **B** silent **C** hesitant **D** nervous

d imputation

A denunciation **B** indication **C** innuendo **D** accusation

e precocious

A sensible **B** cheeky **C** quick-witted **D** advanced

Extension tasks

4 Write your own version of how the story ends. You should use clues and details from the opening of the story and try to write in a style similar to the original.

5 Find a copy of the whole of the original story and read it. Was it what you expected? Did you find it convincing? Why, or why not?

Passage 5

Here is a complete short story. Read it for enjoyment and then answer the questions that follow.

The Necklace

She was one of those pretty and charming girls born, as though fate had blundered over her, into a family of artisans. She had no marriage portion, no expectations, no means of getting known, understood, loved, and wedded by a man of wealth and distinction; and she let herself be married off to a little clerk in the Ministry of Education. Her tastes were simple because she had never been able to afford any other, but she was as unhappy as though she had married beneath her; for women have no caste or class, their beauty, grace, and charm serving them for birth or family. Their natural delicacy, their instinctive elegance, their nimbleness of wit, are their only mark of rank, and put the slum girl on a level with the highest lady in the land.

She suffered endlessly, feeling herself born for every delicacy and luxury. She suffered from the poorness of her house, from its mean walls, worn chairs, and ugly curtains. All these things, of which other women of her class would not even have been aware, tormented and insulted her. The sight of the little Breton girl who came to do the work in her little house aroused heart-broken regrets and hopeless dreams in her mind. She imagined silent antechambers, heavy with Oriental tapestries, lit by torches in lofty bronze sockets, with two tall footmen in knee-breeches sleeping in large arm-chairs, overcome by the heavy warmth of the stove. She imagined vast saloons hung with antique silks, exquisite pieces of furniture supporting priceless ornaments, and small, charming, perfumed rooms, created just for little parties of intimate friends, men who were famous and sought after, whose homage roused every other woman's envious longings.

When she sat down for dinner at the round table covered with a three-days-old cloth, opposite her husband, who took the cover off the soup-tureen, exclaiming delightedly: 'Aha! Scotch broth! What could be better?' she imagined delicate meals, gleaming silver, tapestries peopling the walls with folk of a past age and strange birds in faery forests; she imagined delicate food served in marvellous dishes, murmured gallantries, listened to with an inscrutable smile as one trifled with the rosy flesh of trout or wings of asparagus chicken.

She had no clothes, no jewels, nothing. And these were the only things she loved; she felt that she was made for them. She had longed so eagerly to charm, to be desired, to be wildly attractive and sought after.

She had a rich friend, an old school friend whom she refused to visit, because she suffered so keenly when she returned home. She would weep whole days, with grief, regret, despair, and misery.

☆☆☆☆☆

One evening her husband came home with an exultant air, holding a large envelope in his hand.

'Here's something for you,' he said.

Swiftly she tore the paper and drew out a printed card on which were these words:

'The Minister of Education and Madame Ramponneau request the pleasure of the company of Monsieur and Madame Loisel at the Ministry on the evening of Monday, January the 18th.'

Instead of being delighted, as her husband hoped, she flung the invitation petulantly across the table, murmuring:

'What do you want me to do with this?'

'Why, darling, I thought you'd be pleased. You never go out, and this is a great occasion. I had tremendous trouble to get it. Every one wants one; it's very select, and very few go to the clerks. You'll see all the really big people there.'

She looked at him out of furious eyes, and said impatiently: 'And what do you suppose I am to wear at such an affair?'

He had not thought about it; he stammered:

'Why, the dress you go to the theatre in. It looks very nice, to me ...'

He stopped, stupefied and utterly at a loss when he saw that his wife was beginning to cry. Two large tears ran slowly down from the corners of her eyes towards the corners of her mouth.

'What's the matter with you? What's the matter with you?' he faltered.

But with a violent effort she overcame her grief and replied in a calm voice, wiping her wet cheeks:

'Nothing. Only I haven't a dress and so I can't go to this party. Give your invitation to some friend of yours whose wife will be turned out better than I shall.'

He was heart-broken.

'Look here, Mathilde,' he persisted. 'What would be the cost of a suitable dress, which you could use on other occasions as well, something very simple?'

She thought for several seconds, reckoning up prices and also wondering for how large a sum she could ask without bringing upon herself an immediate refusal and an exclamation of horror from the careful-minded clerk.

At last she replied with some hesitation:

'I don't know exactly, but I think I could do it on four hundred francs.'

He grew slightly pale, for this was exactly the amount he had been saving for a gun, intending to get a little shooting next summer on the plain of Nanterre with

➜

some friends who went lark-shooting there on Sundays.

Nevertheless he said: 'Very well. I'll give you four hundred francs. But try and get a really nice dress with the money.'

The day of the party drew near, and Madame Loisel seemed sad, uneasy and anxious. Her dress was ready, however. One evening her husband said to her:

'What's the matter with you? You've been very odd for the last three days.'

'I'm utterly miserable at not having any jewels, not a single stone, to wear,' she replied. 'I shall look absolutely no one. I would almost rather not go to the party.'

'Wear flowers,' he said. 'They're very smart at this time of the year. For ten francs you could get two or three gorgeous roses.'

She was not convinced.

'No ... there's nothing so humiliating as looking poor in the middle of a lot of rich women.'

'How stupid you are!' exclaimed her husband. 'Go and see Madame Forestier and ask her to lend you some jewels. You know her quite well enough for that.'

She uttered a cry of delight.

'That's true. I never thought of it.'

Next day she went to see her friend and told her her trouble.

Madame Forestier went to her dressing-table, took up a large box, brought it to Madame Loisel, opened it, and said:

'Choose, my dear.'

First she saw some bracelets, then a pearl necklace, then a Venetian cross in gold and gems, of exquisite workmanship. She tried the effect of the jewels before the mirror, hesitating, unable to make up her mind to leave them, to give them up. She kept on asking:

'Haven't you anything else?'

'Yes. Look for yourself. I don't know what you would like best.'

Suddenly she discovered, in a black satin case, a superb diamond necklace; her heart began to beat covetously. Her hands trembled as she lifted it. She fastened it round her neck, upon her high dress, and remained in ecstasy at the sight of herself.

Then, with hesitation, she asked in anguish:

'Could you lend me this, just this alone?'

'Yes, of course.'

She flung herself on her friend's breast, embraced her frenziedly, and went away with her treasure. The day of the party arrived. Madame Loisel was a success. She was the prettiest woman present, elegant, graceful, smiling, and quite above herself with happiness. All the men stared at her, inquired her name, and asked to be introduced to her. All the Under-Secretaries of State were eager to waltz with her. The Minister noticed her.

She danced madly, ecstatically, drunk with pleasure, with no thought for anything, in the triumph of her beauty, in the pride of her success, in a cloud of happiness made up of this universal homage and admiration, of the desires she had aroused, of the completeness of a victory so dear to her feminine heart.

She left about four o'clock in the morning. Since midnight her husband had been dozing in a deserted little room, in company with three other men whose wives were having a good time. He threw over her shoulders the garments he had brought for them to go home in, modest everyday clothes, whose poverty clashed with the beauty of the ball-dress. She was conscious of this and was anxious to hurry away, so that she should not be noticed by the other women putting on their costly furs.

Loisel restrained her.

'Wait a little. You'll catch cold in the open. I'm going to fetch a cab.'

But she did not listen to him and rapidly descended the staircase. When they were out in the street they could not find a cab; they began to look for one, shouting at the drivers whom they saw passing in the distance.

They walked down towards the Seine, desperate and shivering. At last they found on the quay one of those old nightprowling carriages which are only to be seen in Paris after dark, as though they were ashamed of their shabbiness in the daylight.

It brought them to their door in the Rue des Martyrs, and sadly they walked up to their own apartment. It was the end, for her. As for him, he was thinking that he must be at the office at ten.

She took off the garments in which she had wrapped her shoulders, so as to see herself in all her glory before the mirror. But suddenly she uttered a cry. The necklace was no longer round her neck!

'What's the matter with you?' asked her husband, already half undressed.

She turned towards him in the utmost distress.

'I ... I ... I've no longer got Madame Forestier's necklace ....'

He started with astonishment.

'What! ... Impossible!'

They searched in the folds of her dress, in the folds of the coat, in the pockets, everywhere. They could not find it.

'Are you sure that you still had it on when you came away from the ball?' he asked.

'Yes, I touched it in the hall at the Ministry.'

'But if you had lost it in the street, we should have heard it fall.'

'Yes. Probably we should. Did you take the number of the cab?'

'No. You didn't notice it, did you?'

'No.'

They stared at one another, dumbfounded. At last Loisel put on his clothes again.

'I'll go over all the ground we walked,' he said, 'and see if I can't find it.'

→

And he went out. She remained in her evening clothes, lacking strength to get into bed, huddled on a chair, without volition or power of thought.

Her husband returned about seven. He had found nothing.

He went to the police station, to the newspapers, to offer a reward, to the cab companies, everywhere that a ray of hope impelled him.

She waited all day long, in the same state of bewilderment at this fearful catastrophe.

Loisel came home at night, his face lined and pale; he had discovered nothing.

'You must write to your friend,' he said, 'and tell her that you've broken the clasp of her necklace and are getting it mended. That will give us time to look about us.'

She wrote at his dictation.

By the end of a week they had lost all hope.

Loisel, who had aged five years, declared:

'We must see about replacing the diamonds.'

Next day they took the box which had held the necklace and went to the jewellers whose name was inside. He consulted his books.

'It was not I who sold this necklace, Madame; I must have merely supplied the clasp.'

Then they went from jeweller to jeweller, searching for another necklace like the first, consulting their memories, both ill with remorse and anguish of mind.

In a shop at the Palais-Royal they found a string of diamonds which seemed to them exactly like the one they were looking for. It was worth forty thousand francs. They were allowed to have it for thirty-six thousand.

They begged the jeweller not to sell it for three days. And they arranged matters on the understanding that it would be taken back for thirty-four thousand francs, if the first one were found before the end of February.

Loisel possessed eighteen thousand francs left to him by his father. He intended to borrow the rest.

He did borrow it, getting a thousand from one man, five hundred from another, five louis here, three louis there. He gave notes of hand, entered into ruinous agreements, did business with usurers and the whole tribe of money-lenders. He mortgaged the whole remaining years of his existence, risked his signature without even knowing if he could honour it, and, appalled at the agonising face of the future, at the black misery about to fall upon him, at the prospect of every possible physical privation and moral torture, he went to get the new necklace and put down upon the jeweller's counter thirty-six thousand francs.

When Madame Loisel took back the necklace to Madame Forestier, the latter said to her in a chilly voice:

'You ought to have brought it back sooner; I might have needed it.'

She did not, as her friend had feared, open the case. If she had noticed the substitution, what would she have thought? What would she have said? Would she not have taken her for a thief?

Madame Loisel came to know the ghastly life of abject poverty. From the very first she played her part heroically. This fearful debt must be paid off. She would pay it. The servant was dismissed. They changed their flat; they took a garret under the roof.

She came to know the heavy work of the house, the hateful duties of the kitchen. She washed the plates, wearing out her pink nails on the coarse pottery and the bottoms of pans. She washed the dirty linen, the shirts and dish-cloths, and hung them out to dry on a string; every morning she took the dustbin down into the street and carried up the water, stopping on each landing to get her breath. And, clad like a poor woman, she went to the fruiterer, to the grocer, to the butcher, a basket on her arm, haggling, insulted, fighting for every wretched halfpenny of her money.

Every month notes had to be paid off, others renewed, time gained.

Her husband worked in the evenings at putting straight a merchant's accounts, and often at night he did copying at twopence-halfpenny a page.

And this life lasted ten years.

At the end of ten years everything was paid off, everything, the usurer's charges and the accumulation of superimposed interest.

Madame Loisel looked old now. She had become like all the other strong, hard, coarse women of poor households. Her hair was badly done, her skirts were awry, her hands were red. She spoke in a shrill voice, and the water slopped all over the floor when she scrubbed it. But sometimes, when her husband was at the office, she sat down by the window and thought of that evening long ago, of the ball at which she had been so beautiful and so much admired.

What would have happened if she had never lost those jewels. Who knows? Who knows? How strange life is, how fickle! How little is needed to ruin or to save!

One Sunday, as she had gone for a walk along the Champs-Elysees to freshen herself after the labours of the week, she caught sight suddenly of a woman who was taking a child out for a walk. It was Madame Forestier, still young, still beautiful, still attractive.

Madame Loisel was conscious of some emotion. Should she speak to her? Yes, certainly. And now that she had paid, she would tell her all. Why not?

She went up to her.

'Good morning, Jeanne.'

The other did not recognise her, and was surprised at being thus familiarly addressed by a poor woman.

'But ... Madame ...' she stammered. 'I don't know ... you must be making a mistake.'

→

'No ... I am Mathilde Loisel.'

Her friend uttered a cry.

'Oh! ... my poor Mathilde, how you have changed! ...'

'Yes, I've had some hard times since I saw you last; and many sorrows ... and all on your account.'

'On my account! ... How was that?'

'You remember the diamond necklace you lent me for the ball at the Ministry?'

'Yes. Well?'

'Well, I lost it.'

'How could you? Why, you brought it back.'

'I brought you another one just like it. And for the last ten years we have been paying for it. You realise it wasn't easy for us; we had no money.... Well, it's paid for at last, and I'm glad indeed.'

Madame Forestier had halted.

'You say you bought a diamond necklace to replace mine?'

'Yes. You hadn't noticed it? They were very much alike.'

And she smiled in proud and innocent happiness.

Madame Forestier, deeply moved, took her two hands.

'Oh, my poor Mathilde! But mine was imitation. It was worth at the very most five hundred francs! ...'

Guy de Maupassant

Extension task

1 Write a detailed review of this story. You should write about:
- the ways in which the writer has described and presented the main characters
- the setting of the story
- the use of humour
- the writer's use of language
- the way the events in the story develop
- the ending of the story.

2 Would you recommend this story to your friends and would you want to read other stories by the same writer? Give your reasons.

Writing narrative texts

Narrative standpoint

We have already in Chapter 5 looked at personal narratives where the narrator, in the **first person**, is recounting some events from his or her own past life. And we have already established that such narratives do not have to be truly from the narrator's own life, and that a writer can use a first-person narrator where there is no intention of being autobiographical. It is just as likely that the writer will have invented the character who is telling the story and imagined the situations he or she experiences. Choosing to tell a story through a first-person narrator can have many advantages. It means that the story will be told through the words and experiences of a single character ('I') and that the events described can, therefore, only be those in which this character is in some way involved. This approach has the advantage of allowing the reader to identify and sympathise with the narrator quickly and closely and allows the writer to explain the narrator's thoughts and motivations directly. However, it is important for a writer to be consistent in this approach and not to spoil the continuity of the story by including incidents that it is impossible for the narrator to know about.

In a **third-person** narrative the writer chooses to describe the events from an impersonal viewpoint – the narrator has an overall, objective approach to describing what happens and what characters are thinking, and uses third-person pronouns ('he', 'she', 'they') or the characters' names. Such an approach allows the narrator to show a complete understanding of all that happens to all the characters involved in the story – this is sometimes referred to as an omniscient narrative approach – and perhaps allows for greater complexity of structure than a first-person approach. Both types of narrative can be used very effectively when writing a story.

Most examination Writing papers will include a narrative as one of the choices for a student. This is frequently seen by examination students as an attractive option. However, it should not be entered into without thinking carefully. Constructing a convincing and original story on a topic which you have read only a few seconds previously is not an easy task. Many students who choose to write a story as their examination essay do little more than reproduce a half-remembered and not fully relevant story that they have read somewhere before. The best advice is not to attempt to write a short story under limited time conditions unless you feel fully confident that you can do justice to the subject and to your own ability in the time available. On the other hand, writing short stories for your own interest or as part of a class assignment where time is not a constraint can be very enjoyable indeed. Doing so still needs much thought and preparation, however.

Now we are going to look at points to remember when you write an imaginative narrative of your own. We will continue to focus on short-story writing although the techniques required can, of course, be expanded into writing your own novel if that is what you are interested in doing!

Tips for narrative writing

Before writing your story (whether in an examination or at home) it helps to keep the following points in mind:

- Try not to make your story too complicated; remember it is a *short* story and it is a good idea to keep the events tightly focused. You need to engage your readers immediately and ensure that they stay interested throughout. Too complicated a plot is likely to lead to readers becoming unsure of what is happening – this warning applies especially to stories written under examination conditions.

- Try to keep the content of your story to events that are or could be within your own experience. It is much more difficult to write convincingly about things that you do not know. This applies especially to the setting of the story and the situations in which you place the characters. However, there is nothing wrong with taking details of two different places that you know and combining them in such a way that you produce a new, fictional town or village as the setting for your story. It is particularly important that you keep things within your own experience when you write a short story under examination conditions. If your time is limited you don't want to complicate things further by trying to create a completely imaginary landscape, for example.
- Try to break up long sections of narrative with passages of direct speech. Remember that direct speech can be an effective way of lightening a lengthy narrative and can speed up the passing on of information to the reader. However, writing direct speech effectively needs care and thought – you need to be selective about what you decide to put into it and be fully confident in your ability to punctuate it correctly.
- Remember that there are only a limited number of potential plots and situations for any story that you choose to write – it is important that what you write reflects your individuality but that can best be conveyed in the *way* you write. However, if you are writing an examination essay you should avoid uncritically repeating a story you have read or written elsewhere – a memorised story seldom fits the given topic properly, and your attempts to make it do so will always be noticed.
- **Tone/register:** The tone and register you use in your story will help to convey the atmosphere of the story and, in the case of a first-person narrator, the character and personality of the person telling the story. This is another way by which key points can be communicated to the reader in an economical way. The vocabulary and syntax used by the narrator of the story are also effective means of establishing character and the words used may also help to suggest the atmosphere of the events you are describing. Look back at the story of Lena (page 122) and remember how much the language of the narrator contributed to the setting of the story.
- **Conclusion:** It may sound silly, but the first thing you plan should be your ending. Before you start writing you must know where and how you are going to stop. When you plan the events of your story make sure that you have a clear picture of how you intend it to finish. It is up to you whether you want to tie up all the loose ends of your story in a concluding section or whether you intend deliberately to leave your readers guessing what may happen next. Both approaches are perfectly acceptable, but it is important that you, as the writer, have planned the ending – it may, of course come as a complete surprise to the reader!

Punctuation: dashes and hyphens

These two punctuation devices should not be confused. The **dash** is used for a variety of purposes. Its main use is to show where there is an interruption to the intended structure of a sentence, for example when an afterthought is added or an interruption occurs. In these cases, a dash is placed before and after the words that are interjected – unless the interruption occurs at the end of a sentence when it will be concluded with the conventional device such as a full stop, question mark or exclamation mark. For example:

> 'She offered me some of her lunch – and very tasty it was too – before we went back into lessons.'
>
> 'She offered me some of her lunch before we went back into lessons – and very tasty it was too!'

A dash is also used to show when a word or sentence is not completed. For example:

> 'I'll tell you who the murderer is; it was –' a single shot silenced him before he could pronounce the name we had all been waiting for.
>
> 'He was found in the gard –'
>
> 'No, don't tell everyone!' the detective interrupted.

Another use of the dash is to indicate a dramatic pause, usually to draw attention to the end of a sentence. For example:

> 'I'll tell you who committed the murder,' said the detective. 'It was – the mayor.'

A **hyphen** is not really a punctuation mark at all; it is simply a way of linking compound words together (for example, 'the sea was a bluish-grey colour'). It holds the two parts of the word together for ease of reading and avoids possible confusion. Note that hyphens are necessary when using a phrase adjectivally, even if that phrase would not have them when not being used as an adjective. For example:

> 'Please give me the up-to-date figures.'
>
> 'Those figures *are* up to date.'

The hyphen's only other use is as a sign that a word has been split into syllables when there is no space to fit the complete word in at the end of a line of writing, for example 'eat-ing'. In this case, it is important that you place the hyphen between syllables and not between letters at random (for example 'eati-ng'). But better still is to keep an eye on how close to the end of the line you are when writing, so that you move to the next line and avoid using a hyphen at all.

Punctuation exercise

Here is an extract from a short story with all the punctuation removed. Put in the punctuation (including dashes).

> it was very slowly I recovered my memory of my experience you believe now said the old man that the room is haunted he spoke no longer as one who greets an intruder but as one who grieves for a broken friend yes said I the room is haunted and you have seen it and we who have lived here all our lives have never set eyes upon it because we have never dared ... tell us is it truly the old earl who no said I it is not I told you so said the old lady with the glass in her hand it is his poor young countess who was frightened it is not I said there is neither ghost of earl nor ghost of countess in that room there is no ghost there at all but worse far worse well they said the worst of all the things that haunt poor mortal man said I and that is in all its nakedness *Fear* fear that will not have light nor sound that will not bear with reason that deafens and darkens and overwhelms it followed me through the corridor it fought against me in the room I stopped abruptly there was an interval of silence my hand went up to my bandages
>
> From *The Red Room* by H.G. Wells

Narrative writing exercise

Write a story based on one of the following prompts.

1 Title: 'An Unexpected Visitor'
2 Beginning: 'We waited anxiously for five minutes but still no one had emerged…'
3 Title: 'The Old Lady with the Bag'
4 Ending: 'I told you that would happen,' she said.
5 Title: 'The Family Outing'

8 APPLYING READING AND WRITING SKILLS

Having read through the chapters in this book you will almost certainly have realised by now that reading and writing skills are very closely interlinked. Recognising and responding to the features of a particular type of writing when you are reading helps you to produce them in turn when you are writing. Learning how to produce the features in your writing feeds back into your recognition of them in your reading.

In order to respond fully and appropriately to a continuous writing task, it is important that you read the question carefully, consider the topic which has been set and make a direct response to it to show that you understand fully what is required from you. Although the teachers who mark your work will show understanding and not penalise you if, for example, when writing on a topic such as 'Memories of Childhood' (in the plural) you refer to only one memory in your writing, it is very likely (and justified) that you will be penalised if you either misunderstand (or deliberately distort) the given topic and write your essay about 'My Favourite Television Programme' even if the programme was your favourite when you were young.

Similarly, when you are answering a comprehension question or summary task it is important not only that you have read and understood the passage on which the questions are set, but also that you have given equal attention to reading and understanding fully the requirements of the questions that you are answering. It is important to keep in mind, however, that, in an examination, you are only able to communicate your understanding of what you have *read* through what you *write* as your answer. If your writing skills are limited it is quite possible that you will not communicate this understanding fully.

There are some types of examination questions that are marked using both reading and writing criteria. One of these is the summary question, and ways of responding to this have been given in Chapter 4 of this book. Another task which is assessed for both reading and writing is what is usually referred to as a Directed Writing task and this is usually found as part of the Writing paper in most examination syllabuses. It is likely that marks will be allocated equally for both reading and writing. We will now consider ways of approaching this type of question.

Directed Writing

As stated above, Directed Writing tasks (sometimes referred to as transactional writing) test both reading and writing skills. As an examination student, you will be presented with some information relating to a particular topic or situation which you should read carefully, and then you will be required to write a response, using a given genre or format and addressed to a specific audience, through which you show your understanding of the information that you have been given. The task tests your ability to manipulate and focus details from this information and to apply it for a particular purpose, which is stated in the wording of the question. It is likely that the question will contain bullet points that will help you to structure your answer.

The amount of information that you are given varies. In some cases it may comprise just one paragraph and in others the task may be based on a passage of 500–600 words. In the shorter questions, typically, you are told the sort of information to include ('say what happened') but have to create the detail yourself within the scenario of the question. In the longer questions, you are given the detail of what happened and have to use it, maybe from another point of view or for a different purpose. Although the length and type of passage may vary, the basic approach to answering the questions remains similar.

Here is an example of a typical Directed Writing examination question:

> During the lunch-time recess, one of your friends fell over while taking lunch in the school canteen and suffered an injury. It was necessary to summon paramedics and although there were no serious injuries, your friend was taken to the Outpatients' Department at the local hospital to be checked over.
>
> You witnessed the accident and the headteacher/principal of your school/college has asked you to write a report of the incident giving details of what happened.
>
> You should include the following details in your report:
>
> - When and where the accident took place
> - How the accident occurred and the injuries suffered by your friend
> - Suggestions as to how similar accidents can be avoided in future.
>
> You should cover all the points above in detail and ensure that your report is clear and informative. You should write between 250 and 300 words.

The comments below refer to the underlined details in the wording of the question:

- The first paragraph of the question sets the situation or scenario of the incident. It is important to note key details – you are told when the incident happened; that one of your *friends* was involved and that your friend was not seriously injured – be careful here; it's very easy in the heat of the moment to write an account involving seriously broken limbs which does not fulfil the requirements of the question!
- *You witnessed the accident* but you do not have to be involved in it; all that matters is that you saw events at close hand so that you are able to provide a reliable report.
- You are given the genre of what you should write (a report) and the audience to whom it is to be addressed (headteacher/principal of your

school/college). Ensure that you use an appropriate format for your response – a report and not a letter.

- *You should cover all the points above in detail.* For the report to be helpful, it is important that you add some convincing details to the basic facts that the question provides. For example, it is important to give the precise date and time (not just 'last Wednesday during the lunch hour') and also some added detail about exactly where your friend was in the canteen when the accident happened and so on. Note also that the third bullet requires some expansion over and above the information given in the question – a successful response to this question is likely to provide information in response to the second bullet (for example, 'My friend slipped on some food which had been spilled by another student') which can be used when answering the final bullet (for example, 'I suggest that the canteen staff ensure that any spillages are dealt with immediately and that students are directed away from areas where a spillage has occurred').
- It is also important that you stay within the scenario as set out in the question. You may find it helpful to take a few moments to visualise yourself in the canteen and work out what you could have seen or not seen. For example, you could not have seen that the canteen staff failed to clean up the spillage earlier in the morning, even if the failure contributed to the accident.
- Remember the purpose of your answer – this is a report that should focus clearly on the facts; it should be written in a tone that is appropriate to a report and should make its points clearly. In this case your reaction to the events would not be relevant. In a real-life situation it is quite possible that your report could be used as evidence if the school was considered liable for the injuries your friend incurred.

Formats

The example on the previous page was of a question requiring a report. This is not the only format for an examination response to a Directed Writing task. The following are the most common genres that will occur in an examination such as Cambridge O Level English Language:

- a formal letter
- an informal letter
- a speech
- a report
- an article for a magazine or newspaper
- emails.

It is likely that the scenario for the question will relate to the world of study, work or the community and it is expected that the response you write should be fit for purpose if it were to be an actual, real-life situation.

We will now look in more detail at the key features of the different formats.

Letters

Examination Directed Writing questions may ask you to write a letter that could be either formal or informal. The following points should help with how to approach answering in this genre.

- When writing a letter, either formal or informal, as part of an examination question, you will not be expected to include any address (either yours or the recipient's) at the head of the letter so you don't need to worry about this or how to format it. It is likely that the instructions on the question paper will tell you how to begin the letter, for example, 'Begin your letter to the newspaper with "Dear Editor…"'.
- A *formal* letter is one that is written either to someone whom you do not know well or to something such as an organisation, company or newspaper. It is likely to be concerned with putting forward ideas, making a complaint or requesting a particular service.
- Unless you are advised otherwise, a formal letter should begin with the salutation 'Dear Sir' or 'Dear Madam'. It should conclude with 'Yours faithfully' or 'Yours truly' followed by your full name. It may also be necessary to put a brief heading at the start of the letter, after the salutation, if it is appropriate to refer to the topic about which you are writing, for example 'Re: Item lost on number 37 bus'.
- A formal letter should be written in a formal tone so you should avoid colloquialisms and contractions. However, it is not necessary to use business jargon, such as *inst* and *ult* as this is likely to obscure your purpose and also look unnecessarily stilted. It is important that such a letter is clearly focused and logically structured through paragraphs. Remember that in real life, the person reading your letter is likely to be very busy and would want to gain as clear an understanding of your concerns as easily as possible.
- It is not usually appropriate to enquire after the recipient's health, etc. when writing a formal letter.
- A letter to someone who you know, but who you would be expected to treat with some respect, such as a teacher or an elderly neighbour, should also be fairly formal in tone. It should begin by addressing the recipient either by their title ('Dear Headmaster') or their formal name ('Dear Mr O'Grady'). It should conclude with 'Yours sincerely' followed by your full name ('Sam Mendell'). This would be appropriate, for example, if you were writing to Mr O'Grady, who is a teacher at your school, asking him to provide you with a reference for a part-time job.
- An *informal* letter is one written to a relative or friend. It is likely to contain personal information, for example, you may be writing to your grandmother to tell her about a school festival in which you took part.
- You should begin an informal letter by addressing the recipient by name, for example, 'Dear Granny' or 'Dear Lee'. There are no hard and fast rules as to how you conclude an informal letter but your valediction should be in keeping with how familiar you are with the person to whom you are writing. You should sign off with something like 'With love' (for someone you are close to) or 'With all best wishes' (for someone less

close), followed by your first name only. Note that it is not appropriate to use 'Yours sincerely' when writing to a friend or relative.
- It is acceptable to use colloquialisms and contractions in an informal letter although you should not overdo them or fall into extreme teenage slang or 'text language'. It's important to remember that the ultimate audience for your letter is the person marking your work who is trying to assess your competence in writing Standard English!
- Although it is important to keep clearly in mind the purpose for which you are writing the letter and to ensure that your answer is clearly structured and written in paragraphs, it is also acceptable to include some personal concerns such as enquiring about how other members of the recipient's family are getting on, and so on, as long as this does not detract from the overall purpose of the letter. It is best not to use such phrases as 'I hope you are all in the pink of health', however, as such expressions are now outdated and no longer in common English usage.

Speeches and talks

- If a Directed Writing task asks you to write a speech or talk then it is important that you establish an oral register from the start. You can do this quite simply by beginning with a statement such as 'Good morning, everyone; I'm here today to speak to you about ...' and then continue with the points that you wish to make, using the bullet points in the question to help you to structure your speech. You should maintain the oral register by including such things as rhetorical questions and direct addresses to your audience. It is not necessary, however, to include stage directions or anything similar to add to the effect of your speech (for example, *Pause for dramatic effect*).
- As you are writing the words of your speech or talk, then it is perfectly acceptable to use colloquial phrases and even intended non-sentences to achieve an effect. These non-standard English devices should not be overdone, however, because, as always, you will be assessed on how well you can write using Standard English.
- It is important that you are aware of the purpose of your speech or talk and that you adapt the register in which it is given to convince your audience of that purpose. For example, if you are required to persuade your audience to a particular viewpoint, you might well wish to use some emotively toned language to sway their opinions. On the other hand, if your speech is intended to provide information (for example, informing parents of what is needed for students taking part in a school trip), then your language should be more balanced and could well contain examples to illustrate the details that you are providing.

Reports

- As a general rule, reports should be written in a formal register, using plain English, as the primary purpose of a report is to convey essential details as clearly and effectively as possible. Reports should be logically structured and, as with other genres, it is sensible to use the bullets in the question to provide your basic structure.

- It is important not to confuse a report with a formal letter; a report should *not* contain a salutation ('Dear Headteacher', for example) nor a valediction ('Yours faithfully'). There should, however, be some indication for whom the report is intended at the beginning of the report (for example, 'For the attention of ...') and details of the name and position of the writer ('Report written by William Shakespeare, School Captain'). There should be a heading that states the report's purpose ('Report on Accident in the School Canteen').
- As mentioned above, a report should contain only the specific details required; you should adopt an objective tone and avoid falling into narrative or adding unnecessary descriptive details or personal reactions to or speculations about what is being reported. It is acceptable, however, to include recommendations as to further actions to be taken in your concluding remarks – the final bullet may well indicate the need for this.

Articles

- Some Directed Writing questions will ask you to write an article for a publication – this is likely to be a school magazine, a newspaper or some other category of magazine. There are no hard and fast rules as to how to approach writing an article as, to some extent, how you write will be determined by the type of newspaper or magazine stated in the question. If the article is for a newspaper, it is more likely to be intended for a local newspaper than a national or international one as this will allow you to use your own local knowledge and not require you to imagine yourself into a situation of which you have no experience. Similarly, it is likely that the nature of any magazine for which you are asked to write will be kept very general (a magazine for teenagers; a magazine about travel, etc.).
- If you are asked to write an article for a school magazine, those who mark your work will accept a wide range of styles. If your school actually publishes a magazine, then the sensible thing would be to use articles that you have read in that as a model for your answer. If your school does not publish a magazine as such, but issues a regular newsletter to parents then that would be an acceptable format to follow. If you do not have a suitable model, in school, on which to base your answer then it is a good idea to base your article on the style of some other magazine that you read or have access to.
- As a general rule, an article should be relatively informal and clearly directed at the audience for whom it is intended, and which will be specified in the wording of the question. You may therefore include colloquialisms, etc. if appropriate for the audience, but as always don't overdo them. Subheadings may be useful, and features such as rhetorical questions and direct addresses to the audience may also help to produce a lively article that attracts its audience. In an examination answer, it is not necessary to indicate physical format such as columns or pictures.
- You should keep in mind that any article published in any sort of magazine will have been proofread (and corrected) by an editor before it is published. In many schools, a teacher of English will have the position of Editor of the school magazine. Before you write your article, keep the image of your English teachers clearly in your mind; think about what

they are prepared to accept as good writing and what mistakes they would penalise you for in your own writing. If you produce something that you think they would approve of, then it is likely that you have written a successful response.

Emails have so far not featured as a genre in an O Level English Language Directed Writing task but it is possible that they will be used in future papers. If this genre is used, it is still important to remember that one of the main purposes of the Directed Writing question is to assess your ability to express yourself clearly and appropriately using Standard English and therefore much of the advice given about writing letters should also apply to writing emails. Similarly, if an examination question ever requires the use of a blog as a genre, then it would be sensible to base your approach on the advice given above for writing an article.

Practice questions

Letter

You and some friends have recently visited a place of interest (for example, a zoo, an art gallery or museum). Although you all enjoyed your visit, there was one aspect of the visit that you found to be unsatisfactory.

Write a letter to the manager of the place of interest in which you:

- say when you visited the place of interest and why you went
- give details of what you found unsatisfactory and why
- say what you would like the manager to do to improve the situation.

Cover all three points in detail. Your letter should be formal and polite. You should begin your letter 'Dear Manager ...' and write between 200 and 300 words.

Talk

As a senior student in your school/college you have been asked by your principal to give a brief talk on the school Open Day to parents of students who will be starting at the school in the coming school year. You have been asked to inform the parents about how their children should prepare for their first day at school.

In your talk you should:

- say who you are and give brief details of your career in the school
- explain what happens on the first day of a new school year
- say how new students should prepare for the new school and explain to parents what they can best do to help their children.

You should begin your talk 'Good afternoon and welcome to ...'.

Cover all three points in detail. Your talk should be friendly and reassuring as some parents may be worried about what is in store for their children. You should write between 200 and 300 words.

Report

Your headteacher has asked for ideas for a new sport to be added to your co-curricular activities at your school. It so happens that several of your friends and you have recently attended a 'taster' day at the local sports club and tried out several different sports that you had not played before, including one sport that you all found very enjoyable. Write a report for your headteacher stating why you would like this sport to be added at school. Your report must include the following details:

- what the sport is and why you enjoyed playing it
- what the school needs to provide, (for example, a playing field, equipment, qualified instructors)
- what benefit would come to you and the students and the school if you played this sport.

Cover all three points above in detail. You should ensure that your report is clear and informative. You should write between 200 and 300 words.

Article

On your school's Speech Day last week, the prizes were presented by a famous sporting star. You have been asked to write an article for the school magazine describing the event and giving details of the content of the sporting star's speech to the audience at the prize-giving.

In your article you should:

- say when and where the ceremony was held and who the star guest was
- give details of the event and of the main points of the sporting star's speech
- say what you and your friends found most inspiring in the sporting star's speech and why.

Cover all three points in detail. Your article should be lively and should be given a heading. You should write between 200 and 300 words.

Something a little different

The Directed Writing tasks may ask students to write a response based on three bullet points that provide the key points that need to be addressed for a successful answer. The extension task which follows involves a slightly different approach as the points relate to a lengthy passage. When answering it is necessary to show both a clear understanding of the main points of the passage and also to convey an awareness of the character of the narrator. You are asked to show this understanding through the format of a radio interview. Doing this successfully requires the ability to think yourself into the mind of another person. It is unlikely that a format like this will be set as a question for a 1123 Writing paper, but attempting the task is another way by which you can polish your skill in reading for both explicit and implicit meanings.

Before answering the task you might find it helpful to look at these suggestions.

- You should set out your response like a play script, with the person speaking named at the beginning of the paragraph and then the words of what he or she says.
- You should try to develop comments both from the questions of the interviewer and in the replies of the person being interviewed; this is likely to require the skills you have gained from practising argumentative tasks.
- The main focus of your response should be on the replies made to the interviewer's questions, but you should make some attempt to show the interviewer as more than just an anonymous cipher stating the bullet points.
- It may be realistic for the argument to write some quick-fire exchanges in which both characters speak in short sentences or non-sentences, but if you do be very careful also to include some longer, connected paragraphs. Remember that as always you are being assessed on your ability to write correctly in Standard English.
- Remember that the Reading marks in a task of this type focus on your use and development of the material in the passage. For example, try to ensure that everything you make your interviewee say is based on something that you read in the passage. In addition, it is important that, as far as possible, you make some attempt to reflect the personality of the writer, which you should have gained from reading the passage.
- The tone of your response is likely to be informal to suit the nature of the occasion and the comments above about appropriate language when writing a speech or talk apply equally to an interview.

Extension Task

Re-read the complete article, 'Growing Up in Katong' by Cynthia Wee-Hoefer in Chapter 3 (page 30) and then answer the following question.

Imagine you are Cynthia Wee-Hoefer. You are being interviewed on a local radio station about your early life growing up in Singapore during the second half of the twentieth century. Write the words of your interview. The interviewer asks you the following three questions:

- 'Tell me about the place you lived in when you were growing up.'
- 'What did you most enjoy about your childhood?'
- 'In what ways has the area changed since you were young and what are your thoughts about this?'

You should answer all three questions in detail and base your response on information from the passage but not copy from it. The interview should begin with the first question. You should write between 300 and 450 words.

9 PREPARING FOR THE EXAMINATION

Exam preparation

Cambridge O Level English Language is not an examination for which you can prepare by doing concentrated revision consisting of swotting up on key facts because it is not a fact-based qualification. The two examination papers test your ability both to understand something that has been written in English and how well you can express yourself in writing in English. You will not have had the opportunity to read in advance the passages on which you are tested in the reading paper, nor will you know what the topics for writing in the writing paper are before you open the question paper.

So, how best can you prepare so that you do as well as you are able to when you take this examination?

Firstly, it is important that you become fully familiar with the types of questions that the examination might contain and practise answering similar questions consistently over the final two years of your Cambridge O Level course. You can be sure that your teachers will give you plenty of opportunity to do this! This practice is essential in order to achieve examination success – English Language is not a subject that lends itself to concentrated last-minute revision!

Secondly, you should ensure that you are also familiar with what exactly you may be assessed on in both papers as it is important that your responses meet the criteria required for examination success. Again, your teachers will make you aware of these during the course.

Remember, whenever you answer a practice exercise in preparation for the examination, your work on this task is not over once you have completed it and handed in your response for marking by your teacher. Once it has been marked and handed back to you, then it is important to check back through your work and to see how well you did – you can learn just as much from what you did wrong as from what you did right! As far as composition tasks are concerned, you should take note of the errors in punctuation, structure, vocabulary usage and spelling that your teacher has noted in your work and ensure that you know where you have gone wrong and how these errors can be corrected. Your teacher is by far the best resource you have to explain ways in which your work can be improved.

At the end of every term in the years leading up to an examination, it is a good idea to check back over the work you have done which has been marked by your teacher so that you can identify any consistent mistakes that you have made. These could be spelling or punctuation errors that crop up regularly or problems with using paragraphs, for example. Taking the time to do this will provide you with evidence of areas which you need to work on. If you don't do this, these mistakes will become engrained and you are sure to make them when answering questions under examination conditions. In the final weeks leading up to an examination itself, it is a good idea to look back over your record of the most frequent errors you have made so that you are fully aware of them, and can do your best to avoid making them again in the examination room.

The Writing paper

The Writing paper of the Cambridge O Level English Language examination tests your ability to write English accurately and engagingly. You may be assessed on how well you have understood the requirements of the Directed Writing task. It is important with this question that you are fully aware of the audience for whom you are writing and that the tone and register you use are fully appropriate to the task. You must address all of the bullet points on which the question is focused and develop them convincingly and in some detail – simply mentioning them in your response is not sufficient. It is also important that you ensure that you write your response in the correct format (report, letter, etc.) and avoid lapsing into a lengthy piece of narrative writing. Remember that for this task half of the available marks may be awarded according to how well you have fulfilled the content requirements of the question and the remaining marks may be awarded for the linguistic accuracy of your writing.

The second part of the Writing paper requires that you write an essay on one from a choice of five topics (which appear under three headings: Descriptive, Argumentative, Narrative). As part of your preparation for your examination you should have decided which of these three types of writing you are best able to do in response to an unprepared topic under a limited time allocation. Keep in mind, this is not necessarily the type of writing that you most like to do. For example, you may very much enjoy writing short stories but realise that doing so successfully usually involves you in several hours' planning and writing, which you cannot afford under examination conditions. However, although you may not enjoy writing descriptions as much, you know that you are able to answer a descriptive topic more easily in the time available so it is best to choose this topic – you cannot afford to make a false start under examination conditions.

So, spend a few minutes deciding which topic you can do best in the time available – don't just leap in and do the first one on the list because you think that you have to get started as soon as possible. It is important to produce a complete piece of writing of adequate length in the time allowed, but remember that you should also spend some of this time thinking about and planning what you are going to write. Once you have decided on your topic, make a brief plan of what you are going to write; this does not need to be too elaborate – it could just be a list of paragraph topics or a plan in spider diagram form but it is important that you know how your essay is going to finish before you start to write as this will give you a clear conclusion to work towards. Once you have written your plan then try to stick to it as closely as you can. Try to keep to the specified number of words – you may be penalised if you write less than the minimum amount and are likely to penalise yourself if you exceed the upper limit stated.

Your composition may be assessed primarily for its linguistic quality. This does not mean that you will lose a mark for every error of spelling, punctuation and usage that you make but all errors may be taken into account when your work is marked. The greater the number of errors, the more likely it is that your intended meaning will become blurred and the more difficulty the reader will have in understanding clearly what you are trying to say. In particular, failure to separate sentences correctly through the use of full stops is likely to impede clarity of communication, as is the misuse or omission of apostrophes. As far as spelling is concerned, the most serious errors are those of misspelling or confusion of basic vocabulary (there/their, too/to, etc.) or inconsistent spelling of the same word in different lines. You may be excused spelling mistakes in more ambitious and less common vocabulary, especially if the attempted word is particularly suited to expressing the point you wish to convey.

You will gain credit for writing that is well and thoughtfully structured through well-focused and coherent paragraphs, for the use of precise and varied vocabulary and for using punctuation (especially the more sophisticated devices such as semi-colons) in such a way that it helps to control a reader's response to what you have written.

There are two further points to keep in mind when answering (and preparing for) the Writing paper. As mentioned above, you may gain credit for using precise and appropriate vocabulary but this does not mean that you should use all of the longest words you can think of throughout your writing – especially if you are not sure of their meaning! It is more important that you choose the right word for the job, rather than one that sounds more impressive but does not mean what you think it does. Secondly, there is nothing to be gained from learning by heart before the examination a successful essay that you have previously written and then trying to make it fit one of the titles on the examination paper as this will almost certainly result in an examination response that is only marginally relevant and which may be penalised as a result; it may also be seen as an attempt to distort the purpose of the examination which may carry a far greater penalty.

The Reading paper

The Reading paper tests how well you can show your understanding of the passages that are part of the question paper and the questions that are set on them. Remember, that this is a Reading paper and, therefore, you should devote a significant amount of time to reading both the passages and the questions to ensure that you understand the former to the best of your ability and that you are aware of precisely what is the focus of each question before you start to answer – this is particularly important with questions that carry high marks such as a summary.

It is important that you read the passages with your brain fully engaged! It is likely that when you have looked at practice comprehension passages in the classroom, your teacher will have consistently asked you and your friends questions in order to prod you towards a precise understanding of the answers that the questions require. When you are reading the passages on an examination paper, it is a good idea to try to think of the sort of questions that your teacher would ask you about them and then ask (and answer them) in your mind as a way to focus on what is required (but be careful not to ask them out loud in the examination room!).

As this paper tests your reading skills, errors of spelling and punctuation in your answers may not be penalised as long as you have clearly conveyed your understanding of what you have read (although it is best to avoid such errors if possible). Take careful note of questions that require you to use your own words, however, and make sure that you do so as far as possible when answering them (although it is not necessary to paraphrase every word). With questions that do not have this instruction, it is permitted to lift selectively from the passage but the lift must show clearly that you have understood – random, unselective lifting which does not make your understanding clear, may not be credited.

Finally, to return to the point we made at the beginning of this section, Cambridge English Language O Level is not an examination that you can revise for in the conventional way. It is, however, important that you prepare yourself for the sort of questions that you may be required to answer and that you are familiar with what is required when you sit down to start the examination itself. One way you can prepare yourself is to make sure that, over the period building up to your examination, you practise reading such things as newspaper, magazine and other non-fiction articles containing the sort of writing that may feature in the reading passages in a Reading paper – and, when reading these, do your best to read them actively. Reading actively means stopping at certain points and ensuring that you have a clear understanding of what the writer is saying; don't just look at the words and think that you have understood them!

Practice examination–style paper

Writing

Section 1: Directed Writing

[30 marks: 15 marks for task fulfilment and 15 marks for language]

You have recently taken part in a school residential trip to a neighbouring country. You and your friends very much enjoyed the experience and also found it educationally rewarding.

Write a letter to a friend who used to attend your school but who has now moved away to a different part of the country. You know your friend would have enjoyed the trip if he or she were still a student of your school.

Write the letter to your friend in which you:

- say when the trip took place and where it was to
- explain the purpose of the trip and what you did
- say why you found the trip rewarding and what your friend would most have liked about it.

Cover all three points in detail. Your letter should be friendly and lively.

Ensure that your letter is clear and informative. You should write 200–300 words.

Section 2: Composition

[30 marks for language and content combined]

Write on one of the following topics. You should write 350–500 words in total.

Description

1 Describe somewhere that you often visited when you were a young child and say why it was special for you.

Argument

2 'There should be no distinction between boys' subjects and girls' subjects in a school's curriculum.' What are your views?

3 Your school is planning to produce a time capsule that contains various articles that represent your society and which will be buried in the ground for future generations to find. Say which two articles you would include in the capsule and why.

Narrative

4 Write a story that begins or ends with the words, 'I had never even thought about what was inside that shop until that fateful day.'

5 Write a story in which an old notebook and a photograph play a major part.

Reading

Section 1: Reading for Ideas

[25 marks: 12 marks for content, 10 marks for summary writing and 3 marks on short-answer questions]

Read **Passage 1**, *The destruction of the rainforests*, and answer **all** the questions below.

Passage 1: The destruction of the rainforests

1 To many, tropical rainforests are the finest celebration of nature that has ever graced the face of the planet. They are a vivid part of cultures in many lands, contributing to folklore and myths everywhere. Whether as fascinating places on the tourist itinerary or just the backdrop to thrilling adventure films, they provide entertainment for millions. And to the countries in which they are situated, they can bring much-needed revenue, significantly boosting the local economy. Yet they are now at risk. We have already lost half of the world's tropical forests, and the deforestation rate has almost doubled in recent decades.

2 The diversity of life which rainforests support is legendary. In 125 acres of peninsular Malaysia there are more tree species than in all North America; a single bush in Peru hosts as many ant species as there are in the British Isles. As the forests disappear, so too do their species.

Some people argue that if we lost a number of insects yesterday, and the sun still came up today, does it truly matter? But consider the oil-palm plantations of Malaysia: they used to be pollinated by hand. Today they are pollinated by a tiny weevil from the oil-palm's native habitat in West Africa, saving both time and effort.

3 We should also be thankful for the wealth of the tropical forest when we buy a medicine. There is a one-in-four chance that our purchase was derived from tropical forest plants. It may be an antibiotic, an analgesic, a tranquilliser or even cough sweets, among many other products. Medical attention has now turned to the enormous potential of gene therapy, but for the foreseeable future doctors will still need the chemical compounds derived from plants to support their treatments.

4 An important benefit of tropical forests lies with the part they play in climate control. As the green band around the equator becomes transformed into a bald ring, the 'shininess' of the Earth's surface will eventually distort convection currents, wind patterns, and rainfall regimes throughout the tropics, and further afield too. Even more significant is their efficiency as a carbon store, curbing the climatic disruption caused by the build-up of carbon dioxide in the global atmosphere. Emissions of carbon dioxide account for almost half the greenhouse effect, which threatens to bring about drastic climatic and ecological change through global warming.

5 While we benefit, every day, from the existence of tropical forests, we also contribute, every day, to their destruction. People in all developed nations stimulate over-exploitation of tropical forests through their continuing demand for specialist hardwoods such as teak or mahogany, for woodblock floors or fine furniture. Logging has cleared large areas of tropical forest in lowland Cameroon. Hardwood trees of the size to support the rainforest's spectacular diversity of plants and animals take 200 years to grow. In Cameroon and elsewhere there are plans to develop fast-growing hardwoods through genetic engineering, but plantations do nothing to restore the diversity of natural forest.

6 Large areas of the Central American rainforest have been cleared for cattle ranching to supply the demand for steak and beefburgers in North America. In recent years this trade has slowed, but the damage has been done and is irreversible. With no tree cover and no tree roots to retain it, the thin layer of topsoil is almost completely eroded within a few years. In a more indirect fashion, western farmers are contributing to the loss of tropical forest through their unceasing demand for what are seen as cheap supplies of livestock feed. The calorie-rich cassava that feeds European cattle is grown on Thai croplands that have been established on deforested land.

7 Many of the countries where rainforest remains are among the poorest in the world, and the forest and its wildlife are under constant threat from growing populations desperate for land and food. It is hard for governments to resist pressures to 'develop' the remaining rainforest, when so many are in such desperate poverty. Financial aid from more developed countries tends to support the people rather than the natural environment, with the result that too many projects merely accelerate the spread of commercial forestry or facilitate the building of hydroelectric dams to generate electricity, threatening countless square miles of pristine rainforest with flooding. To slow down the rate of destruction, the international community must help rainforest countries develop sustainable management policies and alternative sources of income.

1 a **Notes**

Identify and write down the information from the passage that suggests reasons why it is important to preserve the tropical rainforest, and why it is still being destroyed.

USE MATERIAL FROM THE WHOLE PASSAGE.

At this stage, you do not need to use your own words and may use note form. To help you get started, the first point in each section is given. You will be awarded 1 mark for each content point, up to a maximum of 12.

Reasons why it is important to preserve the tropical rainforest

Example: They are a vivid part of cultures in many lands.

Reasons why the tropical rainforest is still being destroyed

Example: continuing demand for specialist hardwoods

b **Summary**

Now use your notes from **1(a)** to write a summary of why it is important to preserve the tropical rainforest, and why it is still being destroyed.

Use your own words as far as possible. You will be awarded up to 10 marks for producing a piece of continuous writing which is relevant, well organised and easy to follow.

You are advised to write **150–180 words**, including the ten words given below.

Begin your summary as follows:

Tropical rainforests play a vital role in the world because ...

2 Now re-read paragraphs 1–3.

Identify and write down **three** opinions from these paragraphs, each worth 1 mark.

Section 2: Reading for Meaning

[25 marks on short-answer and multiple-choice questions on language]

Read **Passage 2** about how a mountaineer in the Andes finds his way towards safety after a long fall, and answer all the questions below.

Passage 2

1 At the end of the slope the man fell a thousand feet, and came down in the midst of a cloud of snow upon a snow slope even steeper than the one above. Down this he was whirled, stunned and insensible, but without a bone broken in his body; and then in turn came to gentler slopes, and at last rolled out and lay still, buried amidst a softening heap of the white masses that had accompanied and saved him.

2 He came to himself with a dim fancy that he was ill in bed; then realised his position with a mountaineer's intelligence, and worked himself loose and, after a rest or so, out until he saw the stars. Only then did he rest flat upon his chest for a space, wondering where he was and what had happened to him. He explored his limbs, and discovered that several of his buttons were gone. His knife had gone from his pocket and his hat was lost. He recalled that he had been looking for loose stones to raise his piece of the shelter wall. His ice-axe had disappeared.

3 He decided he must have fallen, and looked up to see, exaggerated by the ghastly light of the rising moon, the tremendous flight he had taken. For a while he lay, gazing blankly at that vast pale cliff towering above, rising moment by moment out of a subsiding tide of darkness. Its phantasmal, mysterious beauty held him for a space, and then he was seized with an outburst of sobbing laughter.

4 After a great interval of time he became aware that he was near the lower edge of the snow. Below, down what was now a moonlit and practicable slope, he saw the dark and broken appearance of rock-strewn turf. He struggled to his feet, aching in every joint and limb, got down painfully from the heaped loose snow about him, went downward until he was on the turf, and there dropped rather than lay beside a boulder, drank deep from the water flask in his inner pocket, and instantly fell asleep.

5 He was awakened, to his surprise, by the singing of birds in the trees far below. He sat up and perceived he was on a wide ledge at the foot of a vast precipice, that was grooved by the gully down which he and his snow had come. Heartened by the realisation that life was within reach, he studied his surroundings. Over against him another wall of rock reared itself against the sky. The gorge between these precipices ran east to west and was full of the morning sunlight. The ledge upon which he had come to a halt seemed about halfway down the southern face. Below him there was a precipice equally steep, but eventually he found a sort of chimney-cleft dripping with snow-water down which a determined man might venture. He found it easier than it seemed, and came at last to another desolate stretch of grass, and then after a descent of no particular difficulty to a steep slope of trees on the floor of the gorge.

6 He took his bearings and turned his face up the gorge, for he saw it opened out above upon green meadows, among which he now glimpsed quite distinctly a cluster of strange stone huts. At times his progress was like clambering along the face of a wall, and after a time the rising sun ceased to shine along the gorge, the voices of the singing birds died away, and the air grew cold and dark about him. But the distant valley with its houses was all the brighter for that. He came presently to an expanse of rocky debris, and among the rocks he noted – for he was an observant man – an unfamiliar fern that seemed to clutch out of the crevices with intense green hands. He picked a frond or so and gnawed its stalk and found it helpful.

7 About midday he came at last out of the throat of the gorge into the plain and the sunlight. He was stiff and weary; he sat down in the shadow of a rock, filled up his flask with water from a spring and drank it down, and remained for a time resting before he went on to the houses.

From paragraph 1

3 a What is the 'softening heap of the white masses'? [1]
  b How had it saved the mountaineer? [1]

From paragraph 2

4 What did the mountaineer's intelligence tell him? [1]

5 a What does the writer mean by 'He explored his limbs'? [1]
  b What did the man find out from this 'exploration'? [1]

From paragraph 3

6 a 'He was seized with an outburst of sobbing laughter.'
    What is unusual about the phrase 'sobbing laughter'? [1]
  b What does it tell us about the feelings of the mountaineer at this stage? [2]

From paragraph 4

7 Explain why the slope was now 'practicable'. Give **two** reasons. [2]

From paragraph 5

8 a Why do you think the mountaineer was surprised to be 'awakened … by the singing of birds'? [1]
  b What difference did it make to his feelings?
    Use your own words. [1]

From paragraph 6

9 a The man thinks he is finding his way to safety. Which single word in the first sentence of this paragraph hints that maybe he is mistaken? [1]
  b Give **two** other ways in which the writer makes this part of the man's journey feel threatened. [2]

10 Why did he find it helpful to gnaw on the stalk of the fern? [1]

From paragraphs 1–5 inclusive

11 For each of the words underlined in the passage, choose the option (**A**, **B**, **C** or **D**) that has the same meaning that the word has in the passage.

  a **insensible** (paragraph 1)

  A unconscious **B** unfeeling **C** unthinkable **D** unseen [1]

  b **fancy** (paragraph 2)

  A realisation **B** desire **C** impression **D** dream [1]

  c **phantasmal** (paragraph 3)

  A imaginary **B** ghostly **C** unrealistic **D** fantastic [1]

  d **grooved** (paragraph 5)

  A folded over **B** scratched on **C** hollowed out **D** cut into [1]

  e **desolate** (paragraph 5)

  A bleak **B** wild **C** ruined **D** waste [1]

12 Re-read paragraphs 3 and 5, which contain phrases that tell us about the mountains surrounding the man.

Explain:

- the **meaning** of the phrases as they are used in the passage
- the **effect** of the phrases as they are used in the passage

a 'rising … out of a subsiding tide of darkness' (paragraph 3) [2]

b 'another wall of rock reared itself against the sky' (paragraph 5). [2]

ACKNOWLEDGEMENTS

The Publishers would like to thank the following for permission to reproduce copyright material.

Photo credits

p.16 © wonderlandstock/Alamy Stock Photo; **p.17** *t* © 1997 Siede Preis Photography/Photodisc/Getty Images, *c* © 1997 C Squared Studios/Photodisc/Getty Images; **p.33** © Photodisc/Getty Images/World Commerce & Travel 5; **p.68** © Sion Touhig/Getty Images; **p.96** *t* © Alexander – Fotolia, *l* © Stéphane Bidouze – Fotolia, *c* © avresa/iStockphoto/Thinkstock, *r* © 2010 davidevison – Fotolia; **p.18** *t* © MOKreations - Fotolia, *r* © greenstockcreative – Fotolia, *l* © Stockbyte/Photolibrary Group Ltd/ Environmental Issues DV 48, *b* © Uryadnikov Sergey – Fotolia; **p.98** *t* © Jeremy sutton-hibbert /Alamy Stock Photo, *b* © Joerg Boethling/Alamy Stock Photo; **p.99** *t* © Imagestate Media (John Foxx) / Vol 03 Nature & Animals, *r* © Asianet-Pakistan/Alamy Stock Photo; **p.101** © epa european pressphoto agency b.v./Alamy Stock Photo; **p.103** *both* Image courtesy of People for the Ethical Treatment of Animals, www.peta.org. **p.105** Robert Zehetmayer – Fotolia; **p.106** Christopher Nolan – Fotolia; **p.108** © Karel Miragaya/123RF.

Text credits

pp.9-10 Sri Lanka Visa and Passport Requirements. Retrieved from http://www.worldtravelguide.net/sri-lanka/passport-visa. Used with permission from Columbus Travel Media Ltd.; **pp.14-5** Travelling by bus from www.greyhound.com; **p.17** Why eat 5 a day? from www.5aday.nhs.uk; **pp.24-7** The Amazon: Trip of a Lifetime by Chris Moss, 01 November 2012. © Telegraph Media Group Limited 2006 & 2012; **pp.28-9** Tortello, R.(2001, June 7). 1692: Earthquake of Port Royal. The Jamaican Gleaner. Retrieved from www.jamaicagleaner.com/pages/history/story001.html; **pp.30-2** Growing up in Katong by Cynthia Wee-Hoefer from www.peranakan.org.sg/2011/06/growing-up-in-katong/; **pp.33-5** Onward Virgin sailors by Steve Boggan, 6 October 2007. Retrieved from www.theguardian.com/travel/2007/oct/06/saturday.sailingholidays. Copyright Guardian News & Media Ltd 2016; **pp.36-8** Portrait of the Artist as a Young Dog by Dylan Thomas. Phoenix. Used with permission from David Higham Associates Ltd.; and Dylan Thomas, from PORTRAIT OF THE ARTIST AS A YOUNG DOG, copyright ©1940 by New Directions Publishing Corp. Reprinted by permission of New Directions Publishing Corp.; **pp.47-9** My New Frontier, The Path of A Vegatarian by Linda McCartney, taken from www.newfrontier.com, used by permission of MPL Communications Limited; **pp.50-1** Serve and volley - women are worth the same lolly by Sue Mott, 25 April 2006. © Telegraph Media Group Limited 2006 & 2012; **pp.54-5** Why I Write by George Orwell (© George Orwell, 1933) Reprinted by permission of Bill Hamilton as the Literary Executor of the Estate of the Late Sonia Brownell Orwell; **pp.54-5** Excerpt from " Why I Write" from A COLLECTION OF ESSAYS by George Orwell. Copyright ©1950 by Sonia Brownell Orwell and renewed 1978 by Sonia Pitt-Rivers. Reprinted by Permission of Houghton Mifflin Harcourt Publishing Company. All rights reserved; **p.60** Extract from *Barchester Towers* by Anthony Trollope; **pp.66-7** Animal Testing a Necessary Research Tool for Now by George Poste (Sept. 3, 2006). Retrieved from http://archive.azcentral.com/arizonarepublic/viewpoints/articles/0903poste0903.html . Used with permission from George Poste; **pp.67-8** from www.gan.ca; **pp.68-70** This article first appeared in the Ecologist May 2005. www.theecologist.org; **pp.72-3** A cold, cold Christmas by Martha Jean Baker, 17 December 2007. © Guardian News & Media Ltd 2016; **p.75-8** 'How I Became an Englishman' by George Alagiah, from www.dailymail.co.uk/news/article-401350/How-I-Englishman.html; **pp.79-81** extract from *Cider with Rosie* by Laurie Lee, published by Penguin Random House; **pp.82-4** extract from *The Life and Times of Thunderbolt Kid* by Bill Bryson (2007), published by Penguin Random House; **pp.85-7** *Around the World in 80 Days* by Michael Palin (2010).Used with permission from The Orion Publishing Group, London; **pp.96-7** What are climate change and global warming? Retrieved from http://www.wwf.org.uk/what_we_do/tackling_climate_change/climate_change_explained/. Used with permission from WWF-UK; **pp.98-9** International climate campaign. Friends of the Earth UK. Retrieved from https://www.foe.co.uk/what_we_do/demand_climate_change_23337; **pp.101-4** Courtesy of People for the Ethical Treatment of Animals; www.peta.org; **pp.105-7** Arthur Levine, 'White Knuckles Are the Worst of It', *http://themeparks.about.com* (2003); **p.108-9:** Beverley Fearis, 'Fear is the key on the mother of all thrill rides', the *Observer* (23 May, 2004) copyright Guardian News & Media Ltd 2004, reproduced by permission of Guardian News & Media; **p.112** 2nd T20: Pakistan pull off unbelievable win to take series retrieved from www.dawn.com/news/1197849; **p.113** Courtesy of Ceylon Newspapers (Pvt) Ltd.; **pp.114-5** The Hobbit: The Battle of the Five Armies review – no more than a middling finale from Middle-earth by Mark Kermode, 14 December 2014. Copyright Guardian News & Media Ltd 2016; **pp.122-31** Extracts from 'Seashells' by Curdella Forbes from *Flying with Icarus and other Stories*, published by Walker Books; **p.132-4** *The Door in the Wall* © H.G Wells; **pp.136-42** *The Necklace* © Guy de Maupassant; **p.146** extract from *The Red Room* © H.G Wells; **pp.160-2** SAVE THE EARTH by Jonathan Porritt (Dorling Kindersley, 1991). Copyright © Jonathan Porritt, 1991.

Every effort has been made to trace all copyright holders, but if any have been inadvertently overlooked, the Publishers will be pleased to make the necessary arrangements at the first opportunity.